MW01520866

Further Endorsements for *Hope Realized*

"Bill Holland's book clearly illustrates how EVERY student has a better chance of success when teachers build relationships with them. Holland uncovers this artfully with thoughtful, probing questions presented to four Central Falls High School graduates. While this book is about those students, their challenges and triumphs, it serves as a lesson for all educators — *spend time with every student, show them that you care, instill pride in them and do not give up on any student....it makes a difference.* As Rita Pierson said, '*every child needs a champion.*' Those champions are at Central Falls High School and in every school system across the country."
—Rosemarie Kraeger, Superintendent of Schools, Middletown, Rhode Island, Former President of the Rhode Island School Superintendents Association and Superintendent of the Year

"Bill Holland's latest reflective book about school reform in Central Falls illustrates the essential role that TRUST plays in the chaotic environment that accompanies state intervention. He saw from a uniquely personal perspective that some students survived and thrived if they had a trusting relationship with a faculty member who knew them well and cared. As Central Falls teachers, administrators and parents become increasingly entrusted with important roles in the school, we need to acknowledge that effective school reform efforts must be built on relationships of

mutual trust and respect. Anything else cheats everyone involved as Bill's distilled wisdom makes clear. Read it and learn."
—Ken Fish, Retired Director of School Reform, Rhode Island Department of Education

"Bill Holland's new book is a reminder of the struggles that even talented and motivated underprivileged students experience in pursuing their dream of higher education. As the country moves away from the principles of affirmative action in the 1970's and 1980's, the stories depicted in this book alert us to the need for continued investment and support in developing the diverse workforce of the future."
—Dr. Pablo Rodriguez, President of Latino Public Radio and Former Chair of the Rhode Island Foundation

"Determination and motivation to transform a failing school in order to meet the individual aspirations of disadvantaged students are critical elements for creating change. A never give up attitude by teachers, students, parents, and school board demonstrates that success is achievable no matter what the odds. This book provides real insight for educational reformers for effective change driven by trust and the creation of a new environment that rewards effort and recognizes achievement."
—Dr. James Magee, President of Strategic Innovations in Education, Inc.

Other Books by William R. Holland

The Sealed Truth

A School in Trouble: A Personal Story of Central Falls High School

Selecting School Leaders: Guidelines for Making Tough Decisions

The Making of a School Superintendent: Steve Vander, the Man and the Suit

HOPE REALIZED

....

THE COLLEGE JOURNEY OF FOUR CENTRAL FALLS HIGH SCHOOL GRADUATES

WILLIAM R. HOLLAND

DRAGONFLY PRESS
NARRAGANSETT, RHODE ISLAND

Dragonfly Press
60 Wampum Road
Narragansett, RI 02882

Cover design by William P. Saslow.
Book design and production by William P. Saslow

Hope Realized/ William R. Holland. -- 1st ed.
ISBN: 978-1-312-64551-6

Foreword

In *Hope Realized*, Dr. William Holland takes us along on the exciting journey to success experienced by four minority students from the once troubled Central Falls High School. With the help of caring teachers and administrators, these students found the courage to face their adversities, accept their challenges and achieve their goals. This is a book about the magic that can happen in the classroom when nobody gives up and everyone keeps trying. This is an inspiring book, one that celebrates the dedication of students who have a dream and of the adults who want more than anything to help them achieve that dream.

When Dr. Holland first asked me to write the Foreword to this book, I initially declined. I didn't think I was the right person for the job. After all, I had spent almost my entire teaching career working in suburban schools. In the course of helping him edit the book, however, I had shared with him some pieces I had published on teaching and he assured me that what I had to say about teaching transcended economic and political circumstances. The more I thought about it, the more I realized that he was right. Good teaching, passionate teaching is the same everywhere and, while some of the challenges faced by suburban students may differ from those who struggle with poverty and racial barriers, they nevertheless require the same sort of attentiveness and determination from caring teachers and mentors.

Each fall, all over the country, whether in bucolic country settings, suburban sprawls or amidst urban decay, when high schools open, a diverse population walks through their doors. Some students are enthusiastic and ready for any challenge. Some are frightened and struggling with great insecurities. For some, academic success will come easily and for others, it will be a daily uphill battle. Some leave loving and supportive homes where they will be happily greeted at the end of the day, while others see the school day as a welcome respite from loneliness, neglect, even abuse. And in every school, there are those who will turn to alcohol and drugs to help themselves navigate the choppy waters of adolescence, as well as those who will face prejudice and discrimination from others. The challenges such students face, regardless of the school setting, can hamper the educational process and cause students to shut down.

That is why good teachers wear many hats. They know that teaching is always about more than just getting information out to students and testing them on it. Good teachers work hard to get to know their students; they listen to them and watch them carefully. They notice whose homework habits have changed, who has become suddenly quiet, who seems to be hiding something, who is feeling out of the loop and is easy prey for unhealthy behavior. They prod gently to get to the bottom of problems the students may be facing, school problems, peer problems, problems at home. They provide a listening and empathetic ear and they direct the students to seek and get the help they need. They understand that it is almost impossible to engage hungry, lonely, unmotivated students and so they provide the appropriate nurturing and help that will get the student to a place of learning readiness. And when the students get there, they push them hard to achieve their potential. They find the strategies that will best help each student learn and they challenge them to claim ownership over their own progress. And when the students leave their classrooms, the teachers do not leave the students. They continue to communicate with them, letting them know that their classroom doors are always open, whether for a chat about the game, the school play or for advice on their academic work.

What inspires me most about *Hope Realized* is that Dr. Holland, like every good teacher, does not play favorites. He understands well the different obstacles faced by teachers, administrators, parents, and students and he roots equally for all of them. He knows that success is best achieved when everyone works together and respects the others' needs and contributions. In bringing the stories of these four remarkable young people to light and allowing us to get to know the adults who helped them on their way, Dr. Holland pays homage to the gifts each brings to the other. *Hope Realized* is a celebration of dedicated people working together for a common goal: students who dared to dream, parents and siblings who sacrificed to help them, and teachers and administrators who walked beside them on their inspiring journeys.

Kathleen Pesta
Retired teacher/Author

Dedication

This book is dedicated to the administrators, board members, teachers and students of Central Falls High School who, in 2010, in spite of the incredible strife and agony created by the mass firing of its faculty, have risen from this controversy and are now on a path to genuine school improvement. It is especially dedicated to those special teachers who remained after the firings and continue to inspire their students and get amazing results as they prepare them for further education and a better quality of life.

Contents

INTRODUCTION

....

HOPE REALIZED

Hope Realized: The College Journey of Four Central Falls High School Graduates is a sequel to *A School in Trouble: A Personal Story of Central Falls High School*, published by Rowman and Littlefield in 2010, a book that was classified by *Choice* as "highly recommended" and called "a narrative of hope for all."

This book is more than a book written just for teachers, parents, students, or educators. It will be of interest to anyone who went to college, dropped out of college, or contemplated going to college but never did.

In writing this sequel, I had two main goals. First, I wanted to discover what challenges and obstacles disadvantaged minority students from low income families face and must overcome as they pursue their college degrees. Secondly, I wanted to know how well these students had been prepared for college in view of the fact that they had graduated from Central Falls High School, one of the lowest performing inner city high schools in Rhode Island, a school composed of a large majority of low income Latino families in a small city plagued by concentrated poverty, unemployment, and a myriad of other socio-economic problems.

What makes this story unique is that the students are students from different ethnic backgrounds who graduated from a small high school on the outskirts of Providence that has had its share of national publicity when it fired all its high school teachers and administrators in 2010, an action that was later reversed. The poverty stricken city also received further notoriety when it declared bankruptcy and was under state receivership from 2010 to 2013.

In writing this book, I focused on four graduates from the class of 2009 who went on to college from a high school where more than fifty percent of their classmates had dropped out. I interviewed the students in the spring and summer of 2013 after having periodically tracked their progress during four years of college and asked them to respond to ten questions about their college experiences. I delightfully found that much can be learned from asking a group of past graduates to share their college journeys in their own words, with its highs and its lows, its social and academic challenges, and the important effect it has had on them at this stage of their lives.

The first student is Bryant Estrada who attended Brown University and was valedictorian of his high school class in 2009. A confident and creative young man, he is the youngest child of immigrant Colombian parents and close to his only sibling, an older sister who recently graduated from the University of Rhode Island. Both parents immigrated to Central Falls in the 1980's as young Latino adults. They worked full time and were highly engaged in their children's education. Bryant has battled epilepsy most of his life which he downplays as mild, nocturnal and under control "most of the time."

The second student is attractive and effervescent Theresa Agonia, a former Miss Portugal Rhode Island and popular class leader. Her parents emigrated from the Minho Province in Portugal in the late 1970's. Her father ran a small successful construction business but died suddenly from cancer when Theresa was a junior in high school. In addition to family financial troubles, she has overcome other adversities. For example, after her father's death there was conflict among her relatives over her father's estate that was unsettling to Theresa, her mother, sister, and brother, forcing them to relocate to nearby Cumberland while Theresa commuted in her senior year to Central Falls High. Shortly thereafter, a grease fire badly destroyed their Cumberland house creating a need for temporary housing. Then her mother was laid off from her job causing a loss, not only in salary but also in benefits. The fact that Theresa was a class leader who participated in many school activities and did well in honors courses while holding a number of part time jobs is remarkable.

The next student, shy, soft-spoken, and devout Seventh Day Adventist, Guillermo Ronquillo, came with his parents from Santa Ana, El Salvador in 2002 and entered fourth grade in neighboring Pawtucket schools. Both he and his parents spoke no English at the time. His family moved to Central Falls in 2006 and Guillermo, although by then fluent in English, was misplaced in low level ninth grade classes. Three and a half years later, he finished second in his class, a shade behind Bryant Estrada. According to one of his teachers, "He came from nowhere. His academic excellence went unnoticed at first. He was such a quiet, soft spoken, shy kid who closed his high school career with a real flourish and ended up as class salutatorian."

However, beneath Guillermo's quiet demeanor was a young man driven to be a doctor with the intellect and determination to realize that goal. His father had been an internist in El Salvador but because of his lack of English fluency was unable to pass the physician's licensing exam, a situation that only increased Guillermo's desire to realize his goal to become a medical doctor.

The fourth student, likeable, self-effacing George Carle, was one of thirteen children his birth father had. He seldom saw his birth father who never lived with his mother, Rosa Rosado. Rosa suffered from a bipolar disorder and as a child had grown up in an environment of drugs and violence in a Puerto Rican neighborhood in Providence. As a single parent with three young boys, she had pedaled drugs, been arrested and spent time in prison for physical assault. George, a marginal student, worked just hard enough in high school to remain academically eligible in order to realize his dream of playing college basketball and then later professional basketball overseas.

Rosa moved George and his two step brothers nine times during their elementary school years and on several occasions had to rely on homeless shelters to keep a roof over their heads. After a drug bust in her apartment in 2006, Rosa turned her life around and became a strict and protective mother determined that her boys would not make the mistakes she had made. She also mounted an aggressive campaign to have them obtain their high school diplomas and college degrees. After an academic recovery in his senior year, George was accepted into the Talent Development Program at the University of Rhode Island where he hoped to be a "walk-on" on the basketball team.

Based on the overwhelming obstacles faced by these students, including statistics that demonstrate low college persistence and failure rates of Latino students, especially male Latinos, as well as the specific negative impact of having been products of a high school described as "persistently low performing" that reportedly offered only a "watered down curriculum," the two key questions for this book became: "What were the odds that each of the four students would actually obtain college degrees?" and "How long would successful matriculation take them?"

Four graduates from the Class of 2009
From left to right: Guillermo Ronquillo, Bryant Estrada, Theresa Agonia, and George Carle

Much of the book is organized around ten questions asked of the four students and the responses they gave about their college experiences during the past four years. These responses range from feelings about lack of campus diversity to how well their high school prepared them for college, both socially and academically, to what advice they would give to a group of middle school Central Falls students about the importance of working hard and doing well in school. The insights they share in their own words are particularly meaningful and highlight the critical role that mentors, supportive and engaged parents, siblings and peers, and key faculty and staff play in helping students from urban high schools succeed in college. Interviews with these individuals and the feedback they provide shed real light on what it takes for disadvantaged minority students from inner city schools to persist and obtain their college degrees.

Some people may ask, "Is this book simply about four students who atypically succeeded despite the odds?" The answer to that is a resounding, "No." It is more a case of looking more deeply below the surface at the incredible potential of young people and what they can achieve if given high expectations and personal support from caring teachers, mentors, and parents in spite of social, educational, and economic barriers. Such potential is not confined to a select handful of motivated honors students, rather it is also found in the hundreds of other capable students, many of them with backgrounds like George Carle's, who by nature of their birth and circumstances slip through the cracks, drop out of high school and/or college and face a future without promise.

It has been a joy to follow these amazing young people during the past four years. They have crushed some of the myths associated with minority graduates from a low achieving high school, particularly a high school that has been nationally labeled a dropout factory in a school community where low income, residential instability, and poverty are major challenges and teachers are thought to be below par. However, as of this writing I am pleased to report in Chapter 3 that the high school is on the rebound thanks to the hard work of dedicated teachers, administrators and parents.

William R. Holland

ONE

....

CENTRAL FALLS HIGH SCHOOL

In February, 2010, I had occasion to visit Central Falls High School, a grade 9 to 12 inner city high school with a fluctuating enrollment at that time of just under a thousand students. The school district had been taken over by the state in 1991 because of declining local revenue and its inability to finance its schools. After the district had been run for a short time by the state Department of Education, a school Board of Trustees was eventually appointed with accountability to the commissioner and the Board of Regents for Elementary and Secondary Education, a board appointed by the governor. The governor has considerable influence over the Regents as does the Rhode Island State Legislature, which has final approval of the district's budget.

Central Falls is a densely populated city that measures one square mile with a reported population of slightly over nineteen thousand inhabitants, mainly Latinos, most having emigrated from Central and South America. Situated a few miles north of Providence, Rhode Island, residents share a rich diversity of Latino culture having emigrated from Columbia, Venezuela, El Salvador, Dominican Republic, Panama, and Puerto Rico to name a few of the countries.

In 2010, conditions in the city were not good. Foreclosures were spiking and unemployment was at fifteen percent. As I walked the narrow streets, I saw three and four story tenement buildings boarded up. High school enrollment had dropped by approximately seventeen percent after years of stability. The fiscally strapped city was on the verge of bankruptcy and what later turned out to be political corruption. The combination of poverty, high unemployment, lack of affordable housing and residential instability was causing "families in flight" the coming and going which only added to the language barriers, poor school attendance, and other challenges teachers were facing in their effort to improve student achievement.

Central Falls High School

On the day of my visit, I took a close look at the aging building. It had been nearly three years since I had last seen it and it looked as gray and ominous as ever. There seemed to be a dark shadow covering the front entrance of this 1928 building where nearby three story tenement buildings blocked rays of sunlight from breaking through. Built in a crowded residential neighborhood not far from the center of the small city, there are no playing fields on site and only strips of grass around two sides of the building. The building has truly seen better days. Parents and visitors must park on the narrow streets and teachers and staff must cram into limited parking spaces underneath the building. The only major building project undertaken since its completion had been in 1972 when a library, gym, and classroom addition was completed. I thought, "Here is a case of real inequality, state neglect, and lack of political clout. Why wasn't this old relic razed or at least converted to a low income apartment building years ago? Providence has built new high schools. Why hasn't this happened in Central Falls?"

On August 18, 2006, I had been appointed full time interim superintendent and consultant by the Commissioner and Board of Regents after the previous superintendent left abruptly that July. My deliverables as consultant were to make immediate budget cuts and eliminate a two million dollar projected deficit, prepare a district restructuring plan, and conduct a search for a new superintendent while a No Child Left Behind (NCLB) correction plan instituted by the Department of Education was underway at the high school. Recently retired, some thought I was crazy to accept such an assignment; however, the eight months I spent in Central Falls turned out to be the most fulfilling eight months of my forty-five years in education in spite of what happened after my departure.

When I left the district in the spring of 2007, much had been accomplished thanks to help from a host of consultants and state Department of Education specialists. Block scheduling was in place for the 2007-2008 school year, a student advisory program was underway, and a professional development period had been scheduled within the school day. Perhaps most significantly, with the support of the American Federation of Teachers Union, the Regents, the governor and the Rhode Island Foundation, a partnership contract with the University of Rhode Island had been signed, creating the URI Academy at Central Falls High School, a partnership that focused on high school reform.

Cliff Sylvia, a retired Massachusetts principal, was appointed interim principal that spring, having served as a Department of Education consultant to the high school for the previous eighteen months. A search for a new high school principal was in process allowing new Superintendent Fran Gallo and a search team the opportunity to hire a new leader for the school. And finally, the school received its ten year accreditation from the New England Association of Schools and Colleges having previously been on probation for three years.

Sylvia, in fact, held a series of meetings with the union leadership team and presented a new three phase formative and summative evaluation program for implementation in the 2007-2008 school year for both non-tenured and tenured teachers. A non-tenured teacher evaluation process had already been in place but, to my surprise, tenured teacher evaluation was non-existent, not even on a cyclical basis. I was told by the Director of Human Resources that tenured classroom observations and written evaluations had taken place several years before and were in a separate file in the superintendent's office, but a thorough search of office files turned up nothing. The file was missing and to my knowledge has never been found.

The union, however, was open to discussing a tenure evaluation process with Sylvia but had problems with several of his recommendations, especially the recommendation that department chairs should participate in the formative phase of the tenure classroom observation and feedback process. Although needing further tweaking and not yet approved by the union, a start had been made. The proposed evaluation program had actually been framed, but was placed on hold until the new superintendent and high school principal took charge.

I mention all these details because memories fade and facts often get distorted unless you have been directly involved with the issues. However, at the end of the 2006-2007 school year Central Falls High School was doing well with much hope for the future. What went wrong after 2007 that resulted in the mass firing of teachers and a bitterness that will persist for some time is for others to answer. Although I offered to help in any way I could, I was understandably not asked to return as a consultant to provide assistance. Superintendent Gallo wanted to bring in her own group of educators, people she knew and trusted. I totally understood. Having a past superintendent around would have been problematic for her and for me. It was time for me to move on, but the warm feelings I have for the wonderful students, parents, and teachers of Central Falls have never gone away.

TWO

....

A SAD EPISODE

My purpose in visiting the high school on that overcast day in February, 2010, was to meet with the principal to arrange a school visit for a group of visiting Pennsylvania superintendents. As I approached the school, I spotted English teacher Deloris Grant and ran across the street to renew acquaintances. Deloris had been raised in Central Falls and graduated from its high school. Having moved with her family from South Carolina, her family was the only black family in the city at that time. She understands and identifies with Central Falls students. Known as a teacher who sets high standards and high expectations for her students, she also gets results.

Normally bubbly and enthusiastic, she looked bothered and distressed. Her body language and pained facial expression gave her away. I asked her what was wrong. Near tears, she said, "My little niece asked me today why I had lost my job. I told her I had been fired but was at a loss to tell her why. It broke me up."

Earlier, on February 22, 2010, in a meeting held in the high school auditorium, the Central Falls Board of Trustees had approved the superintendent's recommendation and fired all high school administrators and faculty. Superintendent Gallo would be informing the commissioner that they would be adopting the "turnaround high school model" due to failure to reach agreement with the teachers' union on the superintendent and board's proposed "transformational plan model."

It was a raucous meeting filled with American Federation of Teachers sympathizers in a crowded auditorium where the tension kept building until it was replaced by stinging bitterness and anger as each name was called during the reading of the motion. Several teachers burst into tears, some stood proudly, while others looked defiant. It was truly a sad moment as I sat uncomfortably in my seat looking closely at the concerned faces of the board members and superintendent as the reading of the motion ended and was then approved. I asked myself, "Why did it have to come to this? All teachers, whether competent, highly competent, mediocre, or incompetent were suddenly put in jeopardy and their futures made uncertain. Was this the best solution to turning Central Falls High around and raising student achievement? Where was the evidence to support such a rash action?"

That fateful meeting was followed by further negotiations between Superintendent Gallo and the local AFT leadership to see if the firings could be rescinded with each side making changes in the initial transformation plan preconditions. As the negotiations dragged on, the mass firing vote went viral and received national coverage by both the social media and major news channels. President Obama, Secretary of Education Duncan, Rhode Island Governor Carcieri, and the *Providence Journal* all weighed in and issued public statements in support of Superintendent Gallo and the Board of Trustees' position.

Meanwhile, the AFT counterattacked as local, state, and national leadership joined forces, conducting a rally outside the high school where Jane Sessums, local union president, waved petitions in the air claiming she had hundreds of signatures supporting her union's position. A short time later, over five hundred teacher supporters across the state, surrounded by protestors who wore red high school Warrior tee shirts, descended upon a Board of Regents meeting to voice their protests to Commissioner Deborah Gist and the Regents. The union said they were ready to sit down and resolve the current impasse but it had to be a collaborative process which they felt, up to this point, had not been the case.

All this fighting did not pacify Deloris Grant who was forced to support her union and joined in the candlelight rally with her young niece at her side, despite the fact that she was not by any stretch of the imagination an outspoken, bitter person, or a union activist. I tried to convince her that when she reapplied for her job she was sure to be one of the fifty percent of the current faculty that could be rehired, a process that was outlined in the turnaround federal mandate option. But Deloris was not convinced she would be rehired. With a reported seven hundred teacher applications pouring in from around the country, with a predicted loss in state aid, and with the legal status of contract seniority language still a question, she had lost her sense of security and was emotionally shaken. I wondered how many teachers also felt that their past dedication and accomplishments had been forgotten. According to Deloris, she had to be observed and evaluated by a third party, resubmit an application following specific rubrics and undergo a final interview. She couldn't believe it.

In May, 2010, after four months of bitter warfare and forty hours of negotiations, an agreement was reached that averted the mass firing and saved the jobs of ninety-three staff members.

At the time, I wondered why all this ugly mess had to occur and what long range effect it might have on the high school. My experience told me that many good teachers avoid being active in their union and see it as a distraction to their main concern which is meeting the needs of the students they see every day and, in the case of Central Falls High School, meeting the special challenges of inner city kids.

Many times, but not always, local union leadership is controlled by the same people year after year. This is unhealthy and often leads to a sense of entitlement as leaders become too powerful and entrenched in their positions. This was the case in Central Falls. In over twenty-five years of collective bargaining at the table in five school districts and on the college level, the Central Falls Teachers' Union leadership was by far the most difficult group I had encountered with a steady flow of teacher grievances reaching the superintendent's desk. The union capitalized on an overly detailed contract where many management prerogatives had long ago been negotiated away. They also capitalized on the constant turnover of school level administrators. Granted some of them were weak, but several promising school leaders never had a chance. They got swallowed up, exposed, and blamed for many situations beyond their control. They were frequently constrained by a teachers' contract that gave them little authority. Unprotected by tenure as teachers are, it was a lot easier to demote them, transfer them, or simply not renew their contracts,

The mass firing of teachers raised many questions that resulted in gross speculation and rumors about who was responsible for this ugly chapter in the history of Central Falls High School. Were the superintendent and board placed in an untenable position by the state and federal government? What roles did the new commissioner and the superintendent play? How much did the gridlock between the superintendent and the union president exacerbate this debacle? The fact is the answers to those questions may never be known.

However, one thing is clear. The federal intervention of the Obama mandate of turning around or closing the lowest five percent of persistently low performing schools in the small state of

Rhode Island has to be questioned. The further you get away from the classroom and local and state control and allow the federal government and its bureaucracy to dictate policy and practice, the more you stifle local creativity, adaptability, and choice. The fear of some educators who have experienced the ebb and flow of school reform over many years is that top down standardization will result in mediocrity rather than measureable improvement in student achievement. I share that fear.

Understandably, much needs to be done in our inner cities where minority students are not being properly served and poor student achievement is a national problem. Tenure laws definitely need to be modified so that incompetent teachers can be more easily weeded out as long as they are provided with due process. Tenure should never be for life and teachers and school administrators should be recertified at intervals during their careers. The need for improved tenure evaluation programs should continue to be a state and national priority; however, the actual program should be locally approved and locally developed using flexible guidelines provided by the states.

Past urban school reform initiatives have failed and new approaches are surely needed. But, as one of my colleagues at the time said, "You don't do it by blowing up schools from the President of the United States' office and firing every teacher in the school." As a reliable Department of Education source told me at the time, "The Feds didn't even know there was only one high school in Central Falls until we told them." Unlike Providence and other big cities, teachers can't transfer to other high schools when a school closes. Teachers can't bump middle school teachers either, since most Rhode Island high school teachers don't have certification at that level.

Following No Child Left Behind mandates the Central Falls episode is a prime example of the increased meddling of federal bureaucrats and their questionable attempt to improve teaching by passing mandates with targeted funding. Now here comes the Common Core Standards movement with the goal being to establish a national curriculum. Will alignment with these standards mean better teaching and improved student performance? Or will alignment of the top down standards result in more testing, over-prescribed teaching practices and further time consuming data collection with the end result being rigid methodology and further encroachment on local control?

Don't get me wrong. Standards, evaluation and state assessment are necessary to monitor student progress. Holding public educators accountable is also necessary. Understanding and using that data to improve teaching and learning is imperative. However, without local flexibility and autonomy and the increased fiscal support that is needed, will the achievement gap between urban students of color and white suburban students really be closed? Will high stakes testing as a state graduation requirement really narrow the achievement gap? It hasn't been the answer yet and, in fact, has raised some moral and equity questions that sorely need to be first addressed by educational officials promoting such actions.

As we enter yet another new area of school reform, there are no easy answers. The only thing we can grab hold of is the knowledge that improving the quality of teaching is the key to raising student achievement. We need teachers who are always open to learning and constantly trying to be better at what they do, teachers with high standards who work very hard and are passionate about what they teach, teachers who have high expectations for their students and refuse to give up on any of them, and teachers who are skilled at building the type of student-teacher relationships that are built on mutual respect and caring. They are the answer. The challenge is how to build a school culture, which promotes that type of skill and dedication. Meeting that challenge requires highly competent leadership. This book features some of those talented and skillful Central Falls teachers who possess the qualities outlined above. They are the teachers who have made a difference in the lives of the students featured in this book.

THREE

....

CENTRAL FALLS HIGH SCHOOL TODAY

The November 11, 2013, issue of *the Providence Business News* ran an article entitled, *Report: Central Falls High School Improving*. Two weeks later, a *Providence Journal* article by Linda Borg read "A Welcome Shift at Central Falls High." Other media outlets used phrases like "Turning the Corner" and "Signs of Improvement" as they reported the good news that Central Falls High was rebounding and was no longer the poster child for high school dropout factories.

Very good news came from *The Central Falls High School Third Year Transformational Report* conducted by the Education Alliance and Annenberg Institute for School Reform from Brown University. The report analyzed the results of the high school's implementation of a multi-phase transformation plan adopted in 2010 as the school's response to the state and federal mandate to address those major problems that resulted in the school's classification as one of the lowest "persistently low achieving schools" in the state. The report consisted of data collected from 275 interviews and focus groups of students, leadership, parents, and other community members. It was interesting to learn that forty-one teachers and staff members participated in a focus group or were individually interviewed. The extensive compilation of individual responses of participants to key questions provides an interesting range of opinions and points out general agreement on problems that continued to plague the school such as poor student attendance, a high number of student referrals, and a new student discipline program that many teachers felt was ineffective.

After a thorough reading of the report and talking directly with several teachers, I concluded that the report appeared to be most helpful in providing important information and feedback on the reform activities undertaken by the school during the past three years, while at the same time helping define strategic goals for the future.

The good news was most encouraging. The four year graduation rate had improved from forty-eight percent in 2009 to seventy percent in 2012. Although comparatively still very low, math proficiency had increased from seven percent in 2011 to thirteen percent in 2012. Parent engagement had improved significantly with establishment of a parent training program which has a parent leadership team that meets regularly with school leaders. There is a "parent room" located next to the main office with available resources such as computers, copiers, and phones. In one of my visits to the school, approximately a dozen parents were in and out of the parent room providing a variety of services to staff and students, such as making copies of materials for teachers and typing memos for an overworked front office. The number of busy and involved parents and their enthusiasm was impressive.

A partnership with Rhode Island College was also starting to pay dividends with a series of community programs planned by the college to tap into "the strengths and skills families have and engage them more directly and effectively at the school." One of those programs offers classes for parents in topics ranging from English language to computer skills.

The report also concluded that the climate and culture at the school had improved and quoted such data as a measurable decline in teacher absences and personal days. Teacher responses indicated greater collaboration and communication among the staff. Interestingly, they attributed this change to the stability in administrative leadership after years of constant turnover.

Principal Joshua LaPlante mentioned that he felt that more teachers were engaged in professional conversation than in the past and contributed that to new programs such as the Multiple Pathways program that offers credit recovery and diploma options for potential dropouts and a multi-layered math intervention plan where students get needed extra help in math. With a greater number of students receiving special assistance and graduating, and the possibility of success in the air, more of them are feeling better about their school and their teachers.

Of course, there are undercurrents from some staff members who disagree with the report's findings. When asked what strategies have been most effective in improving school climate and culture, one teacher responded: "There has been no improvement at all in school climate and culture: in fact it is much worse than it used to be three years ago. Restorative discipline practices have been a dismal failure. Attendance and tardiness are huge issues."

In the open ended responses to the question, "In what area do you believe CFHS needs further improvement?" considerable teacher dissatisfaction was expressed with attendance, tardiness, and discipline problems. Chronic student absenteeism since the 2009-2010 school year has actually increased with nearly one out of two students at the high school chronically absent, a ratio substantially higher than the state average. Such absenteeism has been a long term problem in spite of a variety of school initiatives tried over the years and remains a major barrier to increasing student achievement.

A review of the staff comments about the ineffectiveness of the current student discipline system indicates a large majority of respondents felt that the current Restorative Practice/Behavior Management System simply hasn't worked. Student disciplinary issues are extremely high which affects teacher morale and stifles dialogue. Other respondents said there is little or no consequence for disruptive or disrespectful behavior.

The Annenberg/Education Alliance report addresses the discipline problem in its conclusions and states in its first recommendation, "Continue to develop, refine, and communicate behavior management and student attendance protocols and expectations." This recommendation is followed by three other recommendations with the third recommendation being, "Continue to develop opportunities to build stronger relationships between and amongst the various school community stakeholders." The two recommendations clearly are linked together and suggest that the school climate and culture need further attention. In actual fact, as the 2013-2014 school year unfolded, several changes in the discipline system were made and yielded positive results.

In April 2014, I spent a day at the high school observing and talking with school leaders, teachers and with students at lunch, in the corridors, and in class. I realize that my day was just a snapshot of the school as compared to the comprehensive Annenberg report; however, I wanted to get a feel for the school and possibly verify some of my assumptions.

I learned much from my visit and it was generally good news. The appointment of a new assistant principal who was a former teacher in the school has resulted in many teachers feeling that discipline has improved considerably. One teacher who had complained about poor discipline now says, "Troy Silva (new assistant principal) was one of us and someone who understands how to deal with kids and teachers when problems arise with individual students. He is highly visible, empathic and credible, knowing our problems and quickly following up on disruptive students."

As I walked the halls, I again realized how orderly and courteous students were. I have been in hundreds of schools in my years in education and the typical description of inner city schools as rowdy and loud, with administrators roaming the halls with cell phones breaking up fights just does not fit the Central Falls High School I know. Like high schools everywhere, ten percent of students contribute to nearly one hundred percent of the student discipline problems. Those classroom disruptions are caused by students who do not want to be there. Central Falls High now has three separate multiple pathway programs where behaviorally disturbed students and those with severe disabilities are in special support programs and have individualized schedules. The dropout rate has been reduced as a result. It is estimated by the teachers who taught in those programs in the last three years that an average of fifteen to twenty students a year, before the programs were in place, would have dropped out and not have earned their diplomas.

With nearly half of the teachers new to the school since 2010 and many new to teaching in urban classrooms, poor classroom management, according to school administrators, has resulted in some teachers constantly referring students to the principal's office. I was corrected by administrators when I inferred that it was obviously new teachers with this problem and promptly told there were some veteran teachers who have poor classroom management skills that need to be addressed as well. Administrators are working closely with those struggling teachers to help them survive.

I asked Principal Josh LaPlante where the fifty percent of the teachers who left the school had gone. His response was telling. "Many retired, took other jobs, or were terminated. That number includes some non-tenured teachers whose contracts were not renewed." One teacher admitted to me that some forced retirements were overdue; however, the district also lost some great teachers as well, teachers who were quickly hired by other districts.

Superintendent Fran Gallo and Board of Trustees Chairman Anna Cano Morales are still in those key leadership positions with a passion for Latino students and their families as strong if not stronger than ever. The union president, Jane Sessums, still is union president, although now retired from her elementary reading position. Jane and her bargaining group have negotiated two new teacher contracts, not with the superintendent and board, but with Department of Education officials.

Interestingly, Governor Lincoln Chaffee and Commissioner Debra Gist, with support from the state legislature, modified Title 16-2-34(a) of the Rhode Island General Laws after the contentious bargaining that had gone on between the superintendent, the board, and the union in order to mediate the dispute and rehire teachers and adopt changes in the transformational reform plan. The change in the law read, "The Commissioner is authorized to intervene and exercise control of the school district whenever the Commissioner deems such intervention to be necessary and appropriate." This modification in language by the General Assembly and governor in essence has stripped the Board of Trustees of its collective bargaining authority in the last few years and of this writing remains that way.

One could argue that the state is paying the education bill in Central Falls and can exercise any authority it wants. However, if that is the case, then why have a Board of Trustees? If the board is expected to manage and have broad policy making authority for the daily operation of the school district, it must be able to negotiate district contracts in order to counter union attempts to negotiate language it feels is not in the best interests of students. Should not the superintendent and board be responsible for effecting change and increasing student achievement as freely and as independently as possible separate from the political pressure, power, and influence teacher unions have on Rhode Island legislators? Wasn't the board initially established to run the district since they were representative of the Latino population and the needs of Latino students? Are they not appointed by the commissioner and regents and approved by the governor and subject to reappointment or replacement? Why take critical authority away from them?

Quite simply, the board has been reduced to an advisory board without full authority, managing and operating the district on a day to day basis and taking the blame for any problems or failures that occur. Its budget is mainly compiled and submitted by the state Department of Education and regents to the governor and House Finance Committee for approval. It raises the question of continuing to have a board without full authority. If the board's collective bargaining authority is not restored by a new governor, the state may as well revert to 1991 when the state department ran the district and appointed its own state administrator.

In spite of the political problems and persistent problems of chronic student absenteeism and student discipline challenges, the transformation initiative seems to be working at Central Falls High School. The graduation rate is up significantly. The dropout rate decreased by twenty-seven percentage points to fourteen percent which was only two points higher than the state average.

Teacher absenteeism has greatly decreased and is back to normal rates and increased administrative stability is having a positive effect on school climate. Students are feeling better about themselves and their school and there is a new focus on student leadership. Parents are more actively engaged in the school and are making invaluable contributions.

Changes in approaches in professional development are now seen as more relevant and helpful by teachers since they are more directly related to their classroom teaching, thereby helping them achieve success by learning new and useful strategies. As a result, increased professional dialogue can be observed among teachers.

But, much work needs to be done. In spite of small gains in math proficiency, only thirteen percent of eleventh graders reached proficiency in 2012. Math proficiency is a state problem and Central Falls, along with other school districts, is attacking the problem head on. Hopefully, Central Falls with its recent small gain in math scores will continue this upward climb. However, sustainability will be an issue depending upon the success of new math initiatives. Math proficiency should also be evaluated in greater detail on a system wide basis, looking beyond the eleventh grade math assessment score which seems to get all the attention and the bad press. For example, a considerable percentage of eleventh graders may have transferred from other school systems and have not spent the previous twelve or even three years in Central Falls' schools. In this economy with its housing problems, low income families are "in flight" more than ever. The turnover of students from sixth grade to twelfth grade by itself would surprise many researchers. Residential instability of students and families and student absenteeism still are major contributors to low student achievement and are problems of long standing that will not go away quickly. However, the progress the high school has made in the last three years is very encouraging and its commitment to genuine, measurable school reform is laudable. But, those hard working people directly involved admit they will not be satisfied until student test scores reach a much higher level.

FOUR

....

BRYANT ESTRADA

Bryant Estrada always dreamed of going to an Ivy League school. He purposely decided to attend Central Falls High School because he figured his chances of being a top student in his class would be better than they would be if he attended one of the private Catholic college preparatory high schools in Rhode Island. He was right.

Bryant with his family at Brown graduation
Pictured are his dad, Fidel, his mom, Rosalba, and his sister, Michelle

A son of immigrant Colombian parents who valued education (his dad was PTO president) and wanted to see their son become a doctor, Bryant was an exceptional student during his elementary years and eventually became valedictorian of his 2009 graduating class. He decided to attend Brown as a resident student and graduated in 2013.

His college journey at Brown University was a unique experience with its ups and downs, but when I met with him on campus a month before he graduated he was buoyant with a bounce in his step and a wide and welcoming smile on his face. Although he had struggled academically as a freshman, he had finished strong and gained admittance to the University of Pennsylvania's pre-health post-baccalaureate program. He had only positive things to say about Brown and the people along the way who were there to help him succeed—his parents, high school and college faculty and staff, and his sister.

"I always wanted to be a successful person from an underprivileged city," he said. We talked about the fact that he had been placed on academic warning as a freshman and how he had overcome that difficult situation. His explanation reminded me of his college essay when he creatively used a Monopoly game to describe how he sometimes found himself landing on "Chance" and then had to "Go to Jail" as he struggled with his bouts of epilepsy. Now he faced new challenges, like being in academic trouble for the first time in his life, worrying about his college loan debt (Bryant insisted he didn't want his parents to pay for any of his loans), and trying to decide if he really wanted to become a doctor.

Bryant agreed to join Guillermo Ronquillo, Theresa Agonia, and George Carle in responding to a number of questions I had posed about what happened to them during the past four years as they went off to college and what lies ahead as they chart their

Bryant on the steps of Central Falls High School

future courses. The students were asked ten questions and their responses in their own words are included in the pages that follow. But first, what did their mentors think of them?

FIVE

....

BRYANT'S MENTORS

During his four years at Brown, Bryant maintained contact with some of his favorite high school teachers. He felt teachers like Deloris Grant and Doris White were role models and two of the most influential people in his life. They were there to support him prior to college with college applications, throughout college when he needed someone to talk to, and now at the post-college level when he feels the need to talk about what he wants to do with his life. He explains, "I really appreciate all the help they have given me and the dedication that they had to support their students' life goals."

One of Bryant's strengths is his ability to seek out mentors when he needs information, guidance, and understanding. His willingness to "reach out" and get help is exceptional when compared to many other students who wait too long or are afraid to show their weaknesses and vulnerability. He still maintains contact with his high school mentors by visiting them at the high school or arranging to meet them for lunch. His gratitude toward his mentors is obvious as he cherishes the special relationship he has with them and the special bond they share.

Bryant and Dean Besenia Rodriguez

In his responses, Bryant also expresses his gratitude to an Associate Dean and an Assistant Dean who made all the difference in his college transition and eventual success at Brown.

The first lady was Besenia Rodriguez, Associate Dean for Research and Upper Class Studies. Bryant mentions his rough first year at Brown and explains, "I felt like a failure and didn't know where to find help. I needed direction, but couldn't find it. A friend of mine told me about an associate dean who had experience with situations like mine. I went to see her and we automatically clicked. She understood me having been a first generation Latina college student who also had attended Brown, so we related."

"When I first met Bryant he felt a little lost," Besenia said. "He was filled with self-doubt about his abilities and was finding it difficult to adapt to the unique culture at Brown. He was such a promising student with strong family support but was experiencing transition problems that were very similar to the ones I had

34

when I left a city public school and enrolled in a private school. As a result, I immediately connected with Bryant being a first generation Latina who had also attended Brown. No general education requirements or core curriculum, and the fact that students can drop a course one day before finals, creates an unstructured situation that places a premium on student choice. This can be overwhelming to entering freshmen like Bryant."

Besenia found Bryant to be very open and eager for guidance unlike many students who hold back or are resistant to being advised. While he may not have agreed with her on everything, he was very trusting and heeded her advice. She encouraged him to extend his learning beyond psychology and the sciences and to explore other fields where he had special interests.

Following her advice Bryant started to thrive academically and invest himself in the Brown community by participating in a variety of campus activities including joining a fraternity, volunteering at the Third World Center, studying abroad in Denmark for a semester, and joining a dance group. These experiences widened his horizons and created a host of friends that enriched his time at Brown.

When asked how Bryant turned himself around, Besenia explained, "Bryant chooses not to be inward when faced with adversity. Instead he reaches out and opens himself up to others." This ability to make himself vulnerable is obviously how he copes. She continues, "He is honest in a warm sort of way and has a sense of optimism, being never jaded or cynical."

She said she was not surprised about Bryant's decision to drop out of the pre-health program at the University of Pennsylvania. She admits the financial burden is definitely a concern and acknowledges that if he has any doubt about wanting to be a doctor the best time to explore other career options is at the beginning of a medical career. However, she advised Bryant not to close any doors behind him, and to keep his options open. She suggested he take a leave of absence rather than withdrawing after completing his first semester. She told him, "Right now, you may not feel right about becoming a doctor, but a year or two from now, you may change your mind after exploring other career alternatives. There are many ways to help people outside of medicine where you can be happy and fulfilled. You have what it takes to be successful in life whatever career direction you choose."

Mary Grace Almandrez, Assistant Dean of the College and Director of the Third World Center, says this about Bryant: "I met him right after his rough freshman year and knew him well during his last three years at Brown when he was a student staffer who assisted with first-generation student initiatives in our Third World Center (now renamed the Brown Center for Students of Color).

Bryant with Dean Almandrez

"Bryant is a young man of character and integrity. He learned much from the adversity he faced in his freshman year and felt a deep responsibility to reach back and mentor low income minority students who came from high schools like Central Falls High. He quickly emerged as a real leader, someone of influence who can bring people together. He had this strong desire to share his own experience with other first generation students like himself."

Bryant found a home in the center, a place for students of all races, socio-economic classes, genders, and sexual orientations, which Bryant describes as "a safe space for students to share their thoughts and have a place to call their home away from home."

According to Dean Almandrez, Bryant was omnipresent. "I saw him as a person of great passion and heart. He understood how disheartening it can be to fail and face dismissal from Brown. Students were impressed with how he adapted and actually thrived after his freshman year. When he coordinated the First in Family session during New Student Orientation, he packed the room and kept everyone engaged. He gave sage advice on how to navigate the unique culture of Brown and the students listened intently. He was so open and credible."

Bryant summed up his special relationship with her when he wrote, "Dean Almandrez was one of the nicest faculty members at Brown. Greeting everyone with a hug, she gave us warmth, and that was needed greatly, especially at times of stress."

SIX

·······································

BRYANT'S Q AND A

As mentioned previously, each of the four young people was asked a series of ten questions, the answers to which give us major insights and added details, not only into the admirable perseverance of the respondents, but also into what is needed if disadvantaged urban students are to succeed. **The student responses and original works are presented without benefit of professional editing. Typographical errors, however, were corrected.** The first student to respond was Bryant.

How have you changed as a person because of your college experience?

I have changed greatly since May, 2009. I have become more socially conscious, mature, and have learned to solidify my opinions and articulate them well. I am more knowledgeable, and have been able to be exposed to a variety of people from different places with different experiences, which has allowed me to have a better understanding of life. I have discovered my love for being well versed in social issues affecting many minority youth in this country (particularly regarding race, class, gender, sexuality, religion, etc.). I have gained experience working with youth of all ages, as well as adults, and this has helped me with my social interactions, and I have discovered my passion for working with children. I lived away from home for four years, with four months being in another country, and this made me more independent.

Reflect on your college experience. Rate it on a scale from 1 to 10 (10 being the highest). What have been some of the highlights and lowlights?

Reflecting on my college experience, I would give it a rating of 9.5 out of 10. The reason why it is not a full 10 is because of the tough time I had freshman year at Brown, but every year after that was amazing and made up for the difficult times during my first year. Some highlights include: having the opportunity to "be the architect" of my college experience (i.e., being able to choose my classes without restrictions of a set curriculum, taking part in many extracurricular activities, etc.), as well as joining a fraternity (Phi Kappa Psi) which soon after became my family "away" (since not too far) from home. My lowlights primarily took place during my freshman year when I was transitioning into the school both academically and socially. During my first semester at Brown I would go home every weekend, because it was inherently the thing to do, and I think that because I would not spend the weekends at Brown, my social interactions at school were hindered. I did not feel like I belonged. I didn't really feel academically prepared for the challenges that I faced at Brown either. I had a really tough time, but these challenges helped me grow, not only as a student, but also an individual and a liberal thinker. Brown tends to do that to you.

How well were you prepared by CFHS for the challenges of college, both academically and socially? As you look back, which teachers exposed you to experiences and ideas that really made a difference?

Academically

I did do well in college writing papers, all thanks to Mrs. Grant (12th grade AP English teacher), Mrs. Lambert (10th grade Honors English teacher), and Mr. Scappini (Honors US History, AP US History, and AP US Government teacher). They taught me how to analyze text and extract information from the text in order to create a well-written paper. They also accustomed me to read books, with the possibility of these books never being really emphasized during class, and this was way too common in college. Assignments were lengthy for these two English classes and History classes, and these lengthy assignments were difficult during high school, but by the time I wrote a paper during my undergraduate career it was not too difficult to articulate my thoughts well in the assigned paper. I did not feel very prepared for the sciences at Brown. I started taking some science classes at Brown, biology and chemistry, and struggled greatly in both to the extent of failing one, and dropping the other, respectively. I did not know how to study for these classes and stay on top of my readings in order to be prepared for the exams.

Socially

Central Falls High School prepared me for social success. I arrived at Brown and had a tough time at first, but as time passed I was able to find the best of friends based on shared experiences. I was able to find other students with similar experiences in regard to the communities that they were raised in, their races, their socioeconomic statuses, and their types of high schools, as well as their college preparation. The relationships I had with some teachers at CFHS helped me with having great relationships with some professors and faculty at Brown. These teachers, especially Mrs. Grant and Mrs. White, were role models for me. They were both CFHS graduates who were able to do well after high school, and came back to teach at CFHS because they couldn't leave the high school. Even after the situation with the teacher firings, they stayed strong and did not move a muscle. That is what I call determination. That is what I call positive role models.

Remember the charge made that CFHS and other urban high schools offer a watered down curriculum? It was said that honors courses were like regular college prep courses in s good suburban high school. Did you feel adequately prepared as compared to students who came from suburban schools?

I think being in honors courses did give me an advantage over students that were not in these courses, especially because I was able to place into higher-level and AP courses by my senior year at CFHS. Being in honors/AP courses gave me the opportunity to meet some of the most influential teachers in my life. They were able to help me through thick and thin, and prepare me to the best of their ability with the resources that were available to them.

I do feel that I was prepared to be an average student, but not a student who would continue being an "A" student. Though this may be the case, other factors have to be taken into account in regard to this preparation or lack thereof. I think the reason why Central Falls may not be as well-performing as other schools or be preparing their students well for college is because not every student at CFHS goes to college; whereas students who go to college-prep or private schools typically go to college because that is what their school does best, send their students to colleges. Some resources include funding for books. There were times when we wouldn't have books for class (that we could take home), and instead worked with photocopied pages of the book. If the funding was better in the school district, things may have been different.

The recent data shows that Central Falls has improved since our class graduated, and I am proud to see CFHS do better. It is nice to see that they have been able to find an effective strategy to improve the school's overall performance and retention. I hope that this increase in retention and performance continues and CFHS changes for the better.

You have told me that parents, brothers, sisters, past teachers, etc., have played an important role in your college success.

What are some illustrations of the special support and encouragement they gave you?

My Parents

They have played more than an important role in my college success. They have done so many things in their lifetime and in my lifetime that helped my sister and me receive undergraduate degrees. It all started back in the early 1980s when my parents, before knowing each other, came to a totally new country, the United States. They started a new life, all for us, and again this was before they even knew each other. This is a huge sacrifice in and of itself. They knew that they wanted their children to have many opportunities that they did not have the privilege to obtain. Their lives that they created for themselves and their families are a testament to their love for my sister and me, and the desire for us to succeed.

There is one instance during my college career when I felt my parents' support more than any other time in my life. About halfway through my first semester at Brown I broke down in tears in front of my parents. I was having a really tough time: feeling lonely, not doing well academically, and not knowing which way to go for institutional support. Growing up with cultural norms surrounding me which constantly reminded me that it was not socially acceptable for men to cry or show weakness, this was the first time I challenged this norm and it was one of the scariest times in my life. Regardless of this social norm, my parents were there to console me and support me in any way possible. They urged me to let out all of my emotions and that it was fine to show weakness to them, and that it does not take away from my masculinity. Having my parents' support showed me that I can be or do whatever I wanted and that they would be there every step of the way.

My Sister

My sister always tries to give me advice, but no matter how helpful it is, I've always been the stubborn little brother. She has to give me advice; she's my big sister! Her advice is typically in regard to education and career goals, and for some reason, I sometimes don't pay mind to it. It was not until recently that I realized how helpful her advice is. I am currently a student in the post-baccalaureate pre-health program at the University of Pennsylvania. Before going into the pre-medical studies, my sister would always ask me, "Are you sure about this? Are you sure you want to do medicine? Aren't you rushing into things? You just graduated!" Of course, the little brother mentality kicked in and I kept telling her not to worry about it, and that I was definite about the extremely long, expensive career path.

Now that I had the chance to be in the program for a few months, I realized that she was right all along. I woke up one morning and wondered, "Is this actually worth it? Is this worth the financial burden?" I wasn't entirely sure. I have always been interested in mental health, so I have decided to take a break from school, and find a job that will expose me to this field. This was all in the back of my head for a long time, but I guess I never took the time to think about it thoroughly, nor did I accept that this would be the field I would be most interested in.

Past Teachers

All of my favorite teachers supported me every step of the way to getting a college degree. I remember applying to colleges and receiving all of their support. They would stay after school to help their students with college applications, and they didn't think twice about it. I asked Mrs. White for help coming up with a college essay topic. I knew I wanted to make it creative, so of course I went to the art teacher who just so happened to be one of the most influential teachers in my life. She helped me, and there is no way of repaying her for it. I would go to Mrs. Grant so that she could help me with proofreading the essays, and her help was extremely significant to my college applications. She helped me take my essay apart and improve it in order to receive acceptances from the many schools I applied to. I also went to Mr. Scappini to ask him for a letter of recommendation. He didn't think twice about it; he did not hesitate to agree to help me with *this. I think back to this stressful time in my life and the support that they were able to give me during this time, and they are part of the reason why I was able to be accepted to the majority of the schools I applied to, including two Ivy League institutions, Brown University and Dartmouth College, as well as other top-tier universities. I owe it all to them, and I don't know what I would have done without their help and support.*

Upward Bound Counselor and College Crusade Advisor

I was a student in two different college access programs for students throughout Rhode Island who attended high schools that were underperforming compared to other high schools in the state. They helped me every step of the way of the college application process. They helped me with everything from financial aid applications, to college essays, supplements to the college applications, and overall tips for the college application process. There would be times where they would stay late or meet at times when they weren't technically supposed to be working, all to help me. I owe it all to Jessica Rivera and Claudia Erazo-Conrad. If it weren't for these college access programs or these important advisors during my pre-college time, I don't know where I would be right now

Student loan debt continues to be a national problem. Talk about your own financial situation as it relates to the misconception that capable low income minority students have their full college costs paid through financial assistance. Have you had to take out student loans because college costs have exceeded your financial aid package?

Financing a college degree is a struggle. Typically, the schools that will give you the most means of financial aid are usually high performing (private colleges/universities which have a fairly large to huge endowment fund), and, sometimes, are some of the hardest to get accepted to. Low acceptance rates to these universities means fewer students have the opportunity to get the majority of their school tuition covered by the university.

45

Brown University offers a scholarship to students who are first-generation college students and are at the lower end of the lower socioeconomic class. This scholarship, the Sidney Frank Scholarship, is given to students on the basis of need so no application is necessary. Many students do not know that they are "Sidney Frank Scholars" until they are accepted to the University and are given their financial aid package. My experience with scholarships and financial aid at Brown University was different. I did not qualify for the Sidney Frank Scholarship, nor did I apply for any outside scholarships for "misrepresented" students. The only money I had to pay for my education at Brown was what the University gave me in my financial aid package. This was the case for every year except for my freshman year, when I was given outside scholarships that helped me pay for certain educational expenses. At times, I would find myself taking out more loans with the University in order to pay for other educational expenses every year (i.e., books).

Paying these loans off will be a bit tricky. After being at the University of Pennsylvania (Penn, for short) for only a semester in their post-baccalaureate pre-health program, I have decided to take a break from school. A large part of this decision is based on financial circumstances. My time at Penn has been paid off only by loans because the program does not offer any scholarships. I am currently looking for employment back in Rhode Island so that I can start paying the government and Brown for some of the previous loans I took out.

How diverse was your college experience? Describe the typical student at your college. With whom did you hang out? Were there any special programs offered by the college to help Latino and other minority students cope with the change in cultural context?

About half of the students at Brown are white, 10% are international students, and the rest are students of color, so it can be assumed that my college experience was very diverse. I had the opportunity to meet people from all over the world with different stories from my own. I was able to meet many people with intersecting identities in regard to race, class, gender, sexuality, religion, ability/disability, etc. While at Brown I spent time with a variety of people and it enriched my college experience. The people I hung out with were either in my fraternity (Phi Kappa Psi), the dance group I was in (MEZCLA), or the student of color community who were involved with the Third World Center. Among all of these organizations there was a great amount of diversity, with each organization having people from different parts of the world with different intersecting identities in regard to race, class, gender, and sexuality. In terms of special steps, or programs, taken by the university to help Latinos and other minority students cope with the change in cultural context, the university has a center for students who identify with any misrepresented community by race, gender, class, or sexuality.

The Third World Center, established in 1976, is a center that provides a base where these students can have an impact as a community at Brown, and expand social awareness in regard to issues involving the students at the University and the larger society around us (i.e., race, ethnicity, class, gender, differing abilities, heterosexism, and homophobia). By teaching the students about these issues, the TWC prepares students like me with skills that will help them as they navigate their experiences at Brown University, and after they leave the university. Under the TWC exists a residential counselor program, which is specifically to aid students of misrepresented identities in the freshman year dorms, and is called the Minority Peer Counselor Program. The MPCs, who are trained in these social issues, serve as mentors and counselors for students in the freshman dorms who might deal with any of the issues explained above and don't know where else to turn.

The college experience is more than what happens in the classroom. What other learning experiences, both in and out of the classroom, have you had that have contributed to your growth and development in the past four years?

During the spring of my junior year I had the opportunity to study abroad in Copenhagen, Denmark: an opportunity that not many are offered and I am forever grateful for. While in Denmark, I studied Child Diversity and Development to supplement my major. A requirement of the program was a practicum in which I was placed in a classroom in a nearby primary school and was exposed to the Danish education system, which is extremely different from the United States' education system. Education in Denmark has a social development focus through exploration of environment and of self, whereas education in the United States has more of an academic focus where students are constantly tested for their proficiency.

The social development of the education in Denmark goes hand in hand with their way of life: cooperation is the key to success. The support that the Danes have for one another even if they are strangers is fascinating, and I have never experienced viewing this way of being in the United States. The United States is more focused on competition than cooperation, and if this were not the case then no one would be stressing about life. In Denmark it is believed that every profession, no matter how much preparation was done to achieve such position or status, is equal to one another, whereas in the United States there is a hierarchical system of success.

If I wanted to talk to two of your professors, administrators or other educators who know you well and whom you trust and respect, who would they be? How did these people help you?
Dean Besenia Rodriguez – Associate Dean for Research and Upper Class Studies

As stated before, I had a really tough time in college. I was lost at an institution full of college prep grads, and didn't know where to find the help I needed. By the time senior year rolled around, I still felt as if I were

"transitioning." Freshman year was a struggle. By the end of my first year, I was on academic warning, and though I felt like a failure at the time, I soon came to the conclusion that this kind of stuff happens. It helps us grow. I didn't know where to go for help. I needed a direction, but couldn't find it. It was not until a friend of mine told me about a Dean Besenia Rodriguez who had experience with working with these types of situations. I went to see her, and we automatically clicked. She understood me. She knew my experience. Being a Latina first-generation college student who also attended Brown, she related.

Dean Mary Grace Almandrez – Assistant Dean of the College and Director of the Third World Center

Dean Almandrez was there whenever I needed to talk about life. Dean Almandrez might be one of the nicest faculty members that I met at Brown. Greeting everyone by hug, she gave us warmth, and that was needed greatly, especially at times of stress. She was at the time Director of the Third World Center, so she is the one who oversaw the entire Center, including the Minority Peer Counselor Program and the Third World Transition Program. Even with these huge responsibilities, she was dedicated to the students at Brown, especially those who are minorities, not only on the basis of race, but also class, gender, sexual orientation, etc.

You are now a college graduate and in front of you are middle school students from Central Falls. They represent a range of abilities from slow learners to honors type students. A large number have struggled academically; some have a sense of hopelessness because of a trail of failure, while others have done well to date. Most are low income Latino students who are facing socio-economic obstacles outside the school. Many have poor attendance and see little value in school. What do you say to them?

One of the best ways to talk about motivating students is by finding a way to relate with them. Some of these students can relate to Theresa, Guillermo, and me because they are honor-type students, whereas others cannot relate to us in that way. Other students could better relate to George Carle. Some of these students may have dealt with very difficult situations in their life, and a great way to relate is by explaining the adversity that we have all experienced, both during college and before attending our respective universities. Sharing our personal stories of how we overcame and were resilient in these situations may give them the motivation to do better and "get their act together." We can also explain to them that they are still young and that there is still room for change. It is important to show that everyone values their talents and potential for success, and sometimes this isn't really acknowledged so some students may fall through the cracks along the way. I would tell them to keep their heads up. I would explain to them the difficulty of life, but also explain how life will be even harder on them if they do not finish school, especially because of their lack of the opportunities that will be offered to those who have an education and are better off. We need to find a way to make the students feel that they are competent and value their teachers. It would be beneficial to alter their perception of education by explaining positive academic experiences, and the aftermath of these experiences.

SEVEN

....

THERESA AGONIA

Theresa's father died of cancer when Theresa was a junior in high school. To this day, her father's influence remains with her when she says, "I want to be like him. When he died, I felt empty. He is not physically with me now, but he lives in my heart."

Theresa and her late dad, Manuel

Due to a family dispute over her dad's will, Theresa and her family suddenly experienced financial hardship that resulted in their having to leave their home in Central Falls. The family relocated in the neighboring community of Cumberland about the same time her mother was laid off from her job at a local belt factory. Theresa, her sister, and older brother all held jobs in order to pay for family expenses. Shortly after their relocation, a fire occurred in their Cumberland house causing the family to find temporary housing for several months. Miraculously, Theresa managed to graduate with distinction as she commuted to Central Falls High in her senior year.

Facing such adversity, Theresa reached out to her teachers who helped her in a variety of ways, particularly in getting financial aid to the college of her choice, Roger Williams University in Bristol, Rhode Island. She established special bonds with several of her teachers that have continued throughout her college career and beyond. She mentioned much heralded English teacher Michael Occhi who was killed by a drunken driver the summer before her freshman year in college while riding his moped. She indicated that she had leaned on Michael during her father's illness and death and that he had been of immense comfort to her throughout her ordeals. She says, "I will never forget Michael and other teachers who were there for me. "Today, I'm still very close to Deloris Grant, Susan Vollucci, and Ron Thompson and turn to them for guidance or reassurance with decisions I make in my life." Theresa faced adversity and overcame it, never letting life challenges stop her. Her perseverance, tenacity, work ethic and energy contributed greatly to her high school and college success.

Theresa on Graduation Day
With left to right, Mom Fernanda, friend Kayla holding her diploma, Theresa, and
sister, Amanda. Friends Julie and Stacey are in second row

Theresa is also a born leader, a fact supported by her mentors.
Her high school history teacher, Ron Thompson says, "Her attractiveness, engaging personality, initiative, and ability to organize
and lead and getting others to follow her is incredible." Roger
Williams College professor Amiee Shelton supports this conten-
tion when she says, "People respond to Theresa's enthusiasm, energy, and seriousness of purpose. She feels deeply about issues
and her genuineness is obvious."

Theresa exhibits the qualities of passion, credibility, and integrity that characterize successful leaders. In spite of life's setbacks,
she has real self-confidence and poise gained through experience
as a beauty pageant contestant, wherein she was chosen Miss Portugal Rhode Island a few years ago and second runner-up in the
Miss Rhode Island USA contest in 2013. Although totally focused
on a career in communications and public relations, at this point

she feels a responsibility to her mother to live at home and help carry her share of the family's financial burden.

....

EIGHT

THERESA'S MENTORS

Theresa was a work study student for Dr. Amiee Shelton, public relations professor at Roger Williams University. They developed a special relationship as Amiee took her under her wing and introduced her to the world of public relations. They worked collaboratively on a variety of projects, made presentations on public relations at national conferences and invested considerable time in public relations competitions. One noteworthy activity was an anti-bullying project that Theresa initiated in Central Falls schools. The project received national recognition with a ninety-five percent rating in a highly competitive contest.

Amiee describes Theresa as an "awesome" young lady. "She is one of those special students that professors never forget because she has the whole package—amazing charisma, expertise, sincerity, and the power to influence people. At her young age, she has all the key qualities that insure success in the public relations field."

When asked what else sets her apart, Amiee said, "It is her heart. People respond to her enthusiasm, energy, and seriousness of purpose. She feels deeply about issues and her genuineness is obvious. Combine this with her engaging personality and attractiveness, intelligence, advanced communication skills, and growing public relations expertise, she has a very bright future indeed."

Immediately upon graduation, Theresa worked for the Latino Policy Institute at Roger Williams whose director was none other than Central Falls Board of Trustees Chairman, Anna Cano Morales, a woman who knows well of Theresa's ability. In a conversation with Anna she mentioned that everywhere she went with Theresa "someone wanted to hire her." After six months at the Institute, someone else did hire her away. It was the new twenty-eight-year-old Mayor of Central Falls, James Diossa, who hired the multi-talented Theresa as a key person on his new leadership team.

Another key person in Theresa's life is her sister, Amanda, who Theresa calls her biggest cheerleader. Without her support morally and financially she says, "I don't think I would have made it through college. I struggled a lot financially in college and was hesitant to express my challenges to my mom. Instead I always turned to my sister."

Amanda is three years older than Theresa and currently is working as a supervisor for a local restaurant. She was a student at Johnson and Wales University when her father died suddenly. As mentioned previously, his death created an acute financial hardship for the Agonia family. Amanda was forced to leave school and, along with her mother, became a key source of financial support for the family. With the helpful support of KFC franchise owners, Amanda quickly became a manager and then general manager for the company while Theresa worked for KFC in the summers and part time during the school year.

To say that Theresa and Amanda have a special relationship is an understatement. Their sisterly love and unselfish devotion to one another are very apparent. When asked about the sacrifices she has made to help Theresa obtain her college degree, Amanda corrected me. "It was not really a sacrifice because it was my choice and it's what makes me happy. Although older, I look up to Theresa and what she has accomplished. I am proud of the woman she has become. We have a unique relationship that only we thoroughly understand. There's nothing she can't accomplish and I expect her to do amazing things in the years ahead."

Amanda provided an example of how she helped Theresa while at Roger Williams. "My sister never asked me for money, but when I sensed money might have been stopping her from something she wanted to do and should have done, I wanted to support her. She normally doesn't show emotion; however, one day I sensed she was upset because she couldn't afford a student trip to Australia. I was in a position where I could help and I did. The trip was an enriching learning experience for her and it made me feel wonderful that I made her happy."

When asked how she helped Theresa in getting part time employment while in school, she explained, "Theresa has worked for KFC for a number of years even with her busy school schedule. As a general manager, I regularly visited KFC franchises and many times Theresa went with me. When I saw temporary openings, I tried to fit her in a couple of days each week where she could work and make some money."

Amanda remarked that often when they are together, people think Theresa is the older sister. The fact that Theresa is taller and appears very mature, poised, and confident, qualities which were nurtured during Theresa's three year experience as a contestant in the Miss Rhode Island USA pageant, may have something to do with people's misconception according to Amanda.

Theresa
Photo taken for Miss Rhode Island Beauty Pageant

Amanda talks of the dream both she and Theresa share. "Theresa has come so close to winning Miss Rhode Island. I hope she tries again and I really want to see her win. It is my dream as well as hers. She would be a terrific role model for young women," explains Amanda, truly the loving older sister expressing her admiration of her little sister.

Theresa also expresses her gratitude to her pageant coach, Danielle Lacourse of Crowned Inc., who bonded with Theresa since both ladies had witnessed their fathers courageously fight cancer. "Danielle helped change my life. Not only did she serve as my coach during my three attempts at the crown, but she also helped me as a life coach, too."

Ron Thompson is a Central Falls High School history teacher who is currently teaching and advising students in the school's Multiple Pathways program, which provides options for underachieving students to complete their diploma requirements. Along with Deloris Grant, he was Theresa's honors history teacher and one of the teachers she turned to over the years for advice and support. Ron has been called by students, "a teacher you can really talk to" and "so cool he makes you want to learn." When I interviewed Ron, he chuckled and said, "If you want me to I can locate other students who have some less flattering words to say about me." We did agree that his sense of humor goes a long way when interacting with high school students.

When I asked him about Theresa and the fact that she goes to him for support as a trusted mentor, he admitted he had been available to her over the years when "she needed to vent." "Having lost my father at an early age, I connected with Theresa in a special way. She is a great, highly motivated kid who has had to make sacrifices along the way. Her family struggles financially and she feels a strong responsibility to work and ease the financial burden for her mother. It didn't surprise me that Theresa was academically successful in college since she works very hard and as a result is an excellent student. She has amazing social skills and values the relationships she has cultivated during her school years. Her engaging personality, initiative and ability to organize, lead, and get others to follow her is incredible. She is one of those students I will never forget, a truly amazing young lady."

NINE

······································

THERESA'S Q AND A

Theresa had initial social adjustment problems as a freshman at Roger Williams but was quick to adapt to the college culture. She focused on doing well academically and her hard work paid off as she made the Dean's List as a freshman.

How have you changed as a person because of your college experience?

I'm not exactly sure that I would say I've changed since 2009; I'm still the same me. I have, however grown as a person. I've certainly grown as an individual and have become more independent when possible. I've also grown to be more comfortable with myself (this is certainly because of participating in Miss Rhode Island USA). I've even grown professionally. Since the last book, I now am a college graduate. I stayed on track with my communications dream and hold a Bachelor of Arts in Media Communication from Roger Williams University (RWU). I received employment the day before graduation (nerve-racking, I know) and I became a communications assistant for the Latino Policy Institute which is a program of RWU. Presently, I am working as an assistant in public relations for the Mayor of Central Falls.

Reflect on your college experience. Rate it on a scale from 1 to 10 (10 being the highest). What have been some of the highlights and lowlights?

If I had rated my college experience on a scale of 1-10 during my freshman year I probably would have given it a 3. Although I excelled academically, I wasn't having a fun college experience. I wasn't meeting people or being nearly as involved as I had been in high school. Through the years, that changed. I became more involved and met so many great people; people I know will be in my life forever. After four years, I would give my experience at RWU a 10. The amount of learning I did both in and outside of the classroom made me who I am today and I couldn't be happier with that.

How well were you prepared by CFHS for the challenges of college, both academically and socially? As you look back, which teachers exposed you to experiences and ideas that really made a difference?

I believe I was well-prepared for college. During my freshman year, I had a 3.9 GPA. Academically I excelled, but I didn't do my best in other areas. I wasn't as involved as I usually was in school and although I find myself to be rather personable, I found it really hard to relate to people. I was no longer surrounded by people like me, people who grew up in similar situations as me and fighting the same battles as I was. Instead, I was surrounded by people who didn't know what adversity was. That was what I found to be most challenging. Throughout college, I carried a lot of knowledge with me from Mr. Scappini's class. He always made it a point not only to teach us the curriculum, but also to teach us how to survive as well. He made it a point to have 'Life 101' classes whenever we had the opportunity. He helped me get through college more than he knows.

Remember the charge made that CFHS and other urban high schools offer a watered down curriculum? It was said that honors courses were like regular college prep courses in good suburban high schools. Did you feel adequately prepared as compared to students who came from suburban schools?

I don't believe I had good teachers just because I was in honors classes. I believe I had good teachers because good teachers were readily available at my school. The bottom line is there will always be good and bad teachers, just as in any profession (nurses, musicians, actors, police officers, etc.). I'm just fortunate to have had so many great ones. I also feel like I was adequately prepared for college. During my freshman year at RWU I had a 3.9 GPA. If my courses had been watered down, I would not have been able to keep up with my peers. It's all about your own self-motivation. If you want to keep up, you'll make it happen. I'm not saying CFHS is perfect. In fact, I'm saying no school district is perfect; but it's all a work in progress. We need to inch ourselves closer and closer to being better. I challenge the school district with focusing on making curriculum more challenging from the bottom up so all students can continue to push themselves academically.

You have told me that parents, brothers, sisters, past teachers, etc., have played an important role in your college success. What are some illustrations of the special support and encouragement they gave you?

During college, I competed in Miss Rhode Island USA (during 2009 and 2012). I even competed in September, 2013. To help prepare for the pageant I worked with a pageant coach, Danielle Lacourse of Crowned Inc. Danielle helped change my life. Not only did she serve as a coach to me during my three attempts at the crown, but she helped me as a life coach as well. We bonded when we first met over our fathers. My dad had just passed away of cancer and her step-father had recently been diagnosed. It was during my initial consultation with her in Starbucks over a tall iced white chocolate mocha that I knew she would be more than just a coach; she was going to be a friend. When we were training it wasn't just *about me walking away with a crown. It was about me becoming a better Theresa than yesterday and an even better Theresa tomorrow. It's really because of pageantry and working with Danielle that I want to continue to help the community in any way that I can. Each time I inched closer and closer to the crown (2009 semi-finalist, 2012 fourth-runner up, and 2013 second-runner up). Who knows if I'll ever walk away with the Miss Rhode Island USA crown, but what I do know is that I already walked away with a new friend. I also received support during my pageantry from former teachers. Each year I was challenged with raising $700 in sponsorship fees. I had donations from teachers like Deloris Grant, Susan Vollucci, Hope Evanoff, and even from my seventh grade teacher Marjorie McAllister-Hynes. I had great moral support from so many others, too.*

My sister has always been my biggest cheerleader. During college I struggled a lot financially and was hesitant to express my challenges to my mom. Instead, I always turned to my sister. In many ways, I feel so blessed because I felt like I had two moms. Whether it was $10, $100, or advice on a situation, I was always able to turn to my sister Amanda. I don't think I would have made it through college without her support morally or financially. If anyone deserves my degree, it's her.

Student loan debt continues to be a national problem. Talk about your own financial situation as it relates to the misconception that capable low income minority students have their full college costs paid through financial assistance. Have you had to take out student loans because college costs have exceeded your financial aid package?

I was really nervous to take out loans. Knowing that I had no money was a blessing and a curse: it was a curse of course because I never had financial stability but it was also a blessing in so many ways. I always did my absolute best through school because I knew I was paying for school down the line. It was my investment so I had to make the best of it. It also kept me motivated to apply for scholarships. Some students get lazy throughout the four years about fighting for money, but every year I appealed my financial aid package and fought for money I knew I deserved. It always meant something to RWU that a student from an urban city was devoting themselves to the university. It also kept me in classes. I'm paying for each and every class I went to at RWU so I made the best of it. I participated in discussion, always did my assignments, and quite often had perfect attendance. Why? Because I didn't want to waste my money or my time. Though I do have the burden of loans, however, I did have scholarships to help lessen the burden thanks to RWU.

I begin paying my school loans in November, 2013. I'll pay for my loans with every pay check I receive from work. I'm grateful, but I also realize I worked hard to have graduated last May with employment, so I've been able to save throughout these past couple of months. Before I graduated, I never was really able to save money as easily as I can now. I was only working part time while at RWU living on campus so the money I made went to filling my fridge every week, paying bills and paying for opportunities with the school (travelling to conferences, studying abroad, extracurricular activities). Now that I'm establishing myself as a professional in the communications field and have a salary that will increase, I will be able to pay off my loans faster.

How diverse was your college experience? Describe the typical student at your college. With whom did you hang out? Were there any special programs offered by the college to help Latino and other minority students cope with the change in cultural context?

Anyone who says RWU is diverse is, unfortunately, lying. It really isn't. The profile of a typical RWU is a white student, with a lot of money. Unfortunately I didn't know it would be like that before I went to the school so it was a cultural shock when I got there, but life is about learning and embracing your environment. Just because the campus wasn't the diverse crowd I was used to, didn't mean I had a bad time. In fact, I had a great experience there. I did still establish friendships with people of different ethnicities because we all had similar interests, but they weren't the only people I hung out with. RWU is working on their diversity, though. They're working on providing more opportunities for students in urban districts to be able to go to a private university and not feel like it's unattainable to receive a degree from there because of money. That is something I applaud about RWU. They see it is an issue and want to work on improving it. There is an Intercultural Center on my campus (which is where I worked for three years) that is kind of like a hangout spot on campus for the minority students. It has a TV, movies, couches, etc. It was fun to gather there with my friends because no one was judgmental there. In a way, it was like a safe haven for minority students.

The college experience is more than what happens in the classroom. What other learning experiences, both in and out of the classroom, have you had that contributed to your growth and development in the past four years?

The college experience is absolutely more than what happens in the classroom. The best experiences for me occurred outside my classroom experiences. The biggest for me was seeing different parts of the world. During my four years, I had the opportunity to travel to Australia, New Zealand, Fiji, the Whitsunday Islands, the Azores, Portugal, Los Angeles, Orlando, Washington DC, and San Francisco. I practically lived on a plane! During those times, I presented at national conferences, made great friends and memories, and experienced something outside of Rhode Island. It was such a learning experience. I was also able to be a high school mentor for high school students for three years through the Bridge to Success program at RWU. During that time I met so many students in similar situations I was in during high school, students who were facing bigger problems than passing a test - like the fact that they felt they had nowhere to go after school because no one was ever home. It was such a great experience working with students because not only was I able to be a mentor for them but I was also a student and learning from their experiences as well. I was in the Public Relations Student Society of America (PRSSA) as well. It's a student run organization that helps students advance themselves in the public relations field. During my senior year I was named vice-president of the organization after already being part of it for two years. I was presented two awards for my hard work throughout the years - the "Future Leader Award" and the "Exemplary Showmanship in the Field of Public Relations Award". It was great to be recognized for my hard work and to meet great people through the organization.

If I wanted to talk to two of your professors, administrators, or other educators who know you well and whom you trust and respect, who would they be? How did these people help you?

Dr. Amiee Shelton, Professor of Public Relations, Roger Williams University.

Dr. Shelton was my teacher during my sophomore introductory level class in public relations and during my junior and senior year public relations classes. She also became my boss during my junior and senior years. She was my adviser for the organization I was vice-president of during my senior year and part of for three years, PRSSA. She was also my adviser for a national public relations competition I was part of during my senior year. She recommended me to have dinner with President Farish during my senior year on behalf of the Public Relations Department as well.

Needless to say, we spent a lot of time together and got to know each other very well. We even travelled together to Orlando, San Francisco, and Washington DC. Yes, we knew a lot about each other. It came to a point where I could just walk into her office and know right away if it was going to be a good or a bad day. She taught me a lot about public relations. She really kept me interested in the profession and wanting to build the program as much as I did for future classes. We got along so well because we're both fearless. We would rather take a risk than wonder, "What if?"

She helped me learn more about myself as well and really just learn to be a better professional. We still keep in contact and I know I could go to her for any advice with my career or just in life.

Aside from her, I'm still very close to high school teachers Mr. Thompson, Mrs. Grant, and Mrs. Vollucci. I turn to them for guidance or reassurance with decisions I make in my life.

You are now a college graduate and in front of you are middle school students from Central Falls. They represent a range of abilities from slow learners to honors type students. A large number have struggled academically; some have a sense of hopelessness because of a trail of failure, while others have done well to date. Most are low income Latino students who are facing socio-economic obstacles outside the school. Many have poor attendance and see little value in school. What do you say to them?

Ideally, I would love to speak to a group of urban students every day of my life. That's the type of thing I see myself doing down the line. Younger kids need mentors to get through their struggles, especially students in urban cities because they see the most adversity. They need to see people who have come from similar situations that they find themselves in who are now successful. They need to see Viola Davis, Michelle Siwy, and James Diossa and people who have seen what it means to achieve success and continue down that successful path. I would explain to them that it's not easy. In fact, it's really hard. It's hard to remain focused, to not lose hope, and to think you can be one of those success stories, but it's possible. If I were able to get through losing my dad, my mother losing her job, losing the trust I had in many family members and my stability all within a short four month span, success is possible.

I am not an exception to the rule. I am a product of thirteen years in an urban education system and seventeen years in a city. I was able to survive and continue to achieve success because of hard work, determina-

tion and perseverance. Success is a journey and adversity is a mere speed bump on that journey. Sometimes there are more speed bumps on certain parts of the road, but eventually there will be a smooth paved road.

....

TEN

GUILLERMO RONQUILLO

Guillermo is an unusual young man. After reading his college essay four years ago, I marveled at his self-understanding. He knew who he was, where he wanted to go and, most importantly, how to get there.

Guillermo with his dad, Jesus, his mom, Patricia, and his brother, Diego

After arriving with his mother and father from Santa Ana, El Salvador, at age nine with limited English skills, he overcame the obstacles he faced and drew upon his competitive nature, his adaptability, his self-motivation, and his sense of duty to his God and his family. He explains, "My sense of competitiveness and sense of duty are deep within my character, and they only grow stronger as I overcome obstacles in my daily life."

These qualities served him well when, as a quiet and shy young boy entering Central Falls High School as a ninth grade transfer student without any friends, he was, unfortunately, initially misplaced and put in lower level classes. They were also apparent when he worked hard to graduate second in his high school class, and they were there when he confronted discrimination in public places.

His outstanding qualities continued to flourish after he enrolled at Providence College where he received a full scholarship in their challenging honors program. Unfortunately, while playing intramural soccer, he tore both his ACL and MCL and missed the entire first semester of his sophomore year. This did not stop him, however, from finishing his degree requirements in the fall of 2013 as the student with the highest academic record (3.93 GPA) in the Health Policy and Management Program and graduating summa cum laude. And he did it commuting to college for four years in order to save enough money for medical school. Clearly, his dreams and goals were driven by his strong faith, a faith that he says provides the focus that "compels me to do the very best that I can do."

His words of appreciation for the opportunities given him are also telling. "This country has provided fertile ground for me to grow as a better student, a hard working student, and ultimately a success." A success he surely has been and now he is a gifted young man with a very bright future ahead of him. An encounter with Guillermo makes one realize that the American Dream is still very much alive as a prime motivator for low income immigrants and their families. It reinforces the belief that America is still the "Land of Opportunity."

There is another strong motivator that drives Guillermo. His father was an internist at a medical center in Santa Ana but, because of a lack of English fluency, was unable to pass the licensing exam to become a certified physician in the Unites States. As a small boy, watching his dad in his white coat helping people who needed him, he began to aspire to be a doctor himself. It was a dream he brought to the United States where it has grown and magnified to a point where it is now within his reach and ability.

Guillermo with his best friend, Kenny

His father and mother share that dream with their son and together are preparing for the financial challenge ahead. His dad works as an operations manager at a Boston based company that cleans and provides other services for commercial buildings, while his mother works as a child development specialist at a special education center in Fall River, Massachusetts. A younger brother is studying to be a chef at Bristol Community College in Fall River. Guillermo is devoted to his parents and appreciative of the sacrifices they are making to support him and his future dreams.

In responding to the questions given him, Guillermo expresses gratitude to those former teachers who inspired him and prepared him academically for college. Interestingly, the advice he would give to Central Falls' middle school students has a slightly different slant from the advice given by the other three students in this book. Guillermo's mentors also provide excellent illustrations of Guillermo's character, motivation, adaptability and keen intelligence.

....

ELEVEN

GUILLERMO'S MENTORS

One of Guillermo's high school teachers and mentors, Josh LaPlante, made a remarkable observation when talking about Guillermo, "He is an inspiration to me, and it is because of students like Guillermo that I have chosen to remain in education. When all else seems to be discouraging, there are people like him who bring back that emotional connection that brought me into teaching. Guillermo was the type of student that challenged me to be better, and at times he was my 'go to person' for self-evaluation."

High school English teacher, Dolores Grant called him, "A brilliant, creative writer who improved his ability to write with each lesson and strategy given to him." She said it was amazing when she gave him the role of Shylock in the *Merchant of Venice* in the local Shakespearean competition. "His initial cold reading was stilted and his volume too low. He didn't understand the nature of the character. After giving him constructive feedback and time on stage to perform, he improved with each rehearsal, until he achieved perfection to the point where he won awards in the local and state levels."

After his four years at Providence College, I was anxious to contact his college mentors and compare their perceptions of

Guillermo with those of his high school mentors. Two professors who knew him well were Dr. Deborah Levine, his Health Policy and Management advisor and someone he had had for three classes, and Dr. Robert Hackey, the department chair of the Health Policy and Management program who had had him as a student in two classes.

Changing my questioning format somewhat, I decided to ask each professor just three questions. First, I asked them to comment on the preparation of students from an honors program, especially an inner-city program like Central Falls. Second, I asked them what they saw Guillermo doing in ten to fifteen years. Third, I wondered if they thought he might have missed something in his social development by not living on campus for four years.

Dr. Levine's response to the first question was, "I don't feel that I can comment on the Central Falls Honors Program, not knowing anything about it. I can say that Guillermo was usually the best student in any class he was in at Providence College and my colleagues and I often commented on the high quality of his work, especially his written work. It may be that Guillermo is just an exceptional student who would succeed anywhere, or it may be that his high school honors program prepared him exceptionally well, or a combination of both." In a follow-up e-mail, Levine did ask me to pass on her sincere compliments to his English teachers saying, "I wish more of my students had such excellent preparation."

Dr. Hackey also indicated that he couldn't comment on the preparation of honor students from Central Falls, but was most impressed with Guillermo and called him an exceptional student. "I never had a student quite like him. He clearly arrived at Providence College ready to do college level work at a high level."

Guillermo at the Providence College graduation ceremony

Hackey mentioned that the rigor of their highly selective college wide honors program (it enrolls approximately only fifteen percent of the student body) routinely takes its toll on students and their grades. He mentioned that he had taught first generation students prior to his tenure at Providence College, as well as older, more mature students where school to them was a job with an eye on achieving a degree to better their families' circumstances. In those cases, he noted, many students needed to polish up their speaking and writing skills. But when he taught Guillermo, it was different.

Hackey provided an example of Guillermo's superb work when he was in his courses. In his senior year, after Guillermo submitted a major paper in an honors colloquium on health care, Hackey said, "It was the best piece of undergraduate writing I had the pleasure of reading in my fourteen years at Providence College. I encouraged him to submit his paper to a professional journal and at a national conference, because it was already as polished and professional as many conference presentations and papers I've seen in recent years.

"I think his greatest strength is something that can't be taught and that is a drive to succeed, and a tenaciousness than simply won't quit. This, more than anything else, will ensure that he has a successful future."

In response to the second question, Dr. Levine felt confident that whatever Guillermo decides to do career-wise during the next ten to fifteen years, he will be successful. "He would make an excellent doctor, but he also excelled in our health policy curriculum and I wouldn't be surprised to see him involved in business or in politics related to health care as his career progresses."

Hackey also was confident that Guillermo would thrive in whatever task he sets out to accomplish. He elaborates further, "His desire to go to medical school is palpable, and I am sure that he will. I'm also convinced, however, that his gift for writing will not fall by the wayside. I expect that he will also feed his creative side, becoming a physician/author. He will be a compassionate physician who will have a lot to say about both how doctors practice medicine and how well medicine lives up to its promise for patients."

Both professors had similar thoughts on the third question about what effect, if any, did Guillermo's not living on campus have on his social development. Dr. Levine mentioned that on-campus social culture at college these days is too oriented around alcohol and binge drinking. She relates a conversation she had with Guillermo about how difficult it was to find social activities that were not organized around drinking. "As a Seventh Day Adventist and a devoted student, binge drinking was not on his to-do list. So even though I think Guillermo might have gained some important life experiences from living on campus, he always seemed engaged, busy, and well-liked by his fellow students despite his status as a commuter."

Dr. Hackey shares his colleague's opinion, "I don't think Guillermo missed much. Our college has a well-deserved reputation as a 'party school' because our students work hard but play hard. I know that Guillermo contemplated transferring to another school during his first year. This was simply not Guillermo's social scene, so I think his decision to commute and remain centered in his church and community was a wise one. He is still somewhat shy and reserved, but has developed a quiet confidence over time. In my view, he is well adjusted, with a clear sense of who he is. Living on campus is a wonderful experience for many students, but it often comes with challenges in terms of balancing social life with academics. Guillermo's decision to commute put the emphasis squarely on his academics. His earnest, genuine character shines through regardless of where he lived as a student."

TWELVE

....

GUILLERMO'S Q AND A

Guillermo commuted to Providence College for four years while the three other students lived on campuses at their respective colleges. He received a full honors scholarship allowing him to pursue his long term goal of becoming a doctor. As he mentions, his increased confidence resulted in a corresponding growth in his social, interpersonal, and intellectual success.

How have you changed as a person because of your college experience?

I changed in three important ways. I have gained greater confidence, both in my ability to understand higher level materials and to handle a busy schedule. I have gained greater interpersonal skills. In high school I was very shy and almost never participated in class. Going through the honors program which emphasizes group projects and seminar style discussions has helped me with this. I have also learned to be a little more selfish about my health. While getting good grades is important to me, I have learned to make time for exercise, sleep, and recreation. I have achieved this by learning to be more productive with my time.

81

Reflect on your college experience. Rate it on a scale from 1 to 10 (10 being the highest). What have been some of the highlights and lowlights?

    a.   *One of the more disappointing experiences at PC was my injury. I regret having to take the semester off and delay my graduation. Other than that, I have loved my college experience.*

    b.   *One of the things I loved the most was PC's core requirements. Though I may have complained about them as I was going through them, I now see their value. The honors courses, for example, not only made me a more culturally aware person, but have also made me a better reader, writer, and communicator.*

How well were you prepared by CFHS for the challenges of college, both academically and socially? As you look back, which teachers exposed you to experiences and ideas that really made a difference?

    a.   *I believe I was well prepared. I only received one bad grade in my entire four years, and still managed to bring that grade up to an A. I had a B in Art, but that was just because my professor did not see my creative genius.*

    b.   *Mr. Laplante's enthusiasm for the life sciences and creative teaching style was one of the main reasons why I love science. He was also very good about instilling confidence in students, both by holding them up to high standards and helping them when they needed help. He always had an open door policy, whether for academic help, to chat about personal difficulties, or to help out with college applications.*

    c.   *Mrs. Grant was very passionate about her career and teaching students. It was in her AP English class that I truly developed my reading and writing skills which, in turn, helped me throughout college. I'll always remember winning the Shake-*

speare competition. She was able to take the shyest kid in class (probably in the school) and motivate him to go on to win the whole thing. I don't know how she got that out of me, but I thank her. It was a major step in coming out of my shell and developing my social and interpersonal skills.

d. Mrs. Lambert. She was an interesting teacher. Neither I nor Bryant remembered her when the first version of this book was being written. She was not very popular with the students. This was probably because she was a hard teacher. However, during a recent conversation with Bryant we realized that she was the one that had the highest standards for the honors group and the skills that she taught us were most relevant for college. These include:

1. Writing exercises where she introduced a prompt and we only had five to ten minutes. I have used this skill many times during exams. Some exams are made up of eight essay questions, for example, and you have to be able to recall information and get it down within one hour.

2. Formal essay assignments that we revised multiple times

3. Seminar style discussions of the books we read.

4. Reading long books in a very short period of time. Sometimes we didn't even have time to go over them at all during lectures, just like college.

It is very unfortunate we did not remember her. I would like to reach out and say thank you. Though she may not have been popular at the time, I now see why she taught the way she did.

Remember the charge made that CFHS and other urban high schools offer a watered down curriculum? It was said that honors courses were like regular college prep courses in a good suburban high school. Did you feel adequately prepared as compared to students who came from suburban schools?

    a.   *I always felt challenged in high school. There was one math class that I thought was very easy freshman year, but then was transferred to the honors Algebra class within the month so I did not have enough experience in the easier class to make a judgment.*

    b.   *In comparison to my college classmates who went to private schools I outperformed many of them. I had the highest academic record in my major and graduated from the honors program.*

You have told me that parents, brothers, sisters, past teachers, etc., have played an important role in your college success. What are some illustrations of the special support and encouragement they gave me?

    a.   *They have helped me pay for books.*

    b.   *They paid for my surgery and rehabilitation. My mom took time off of work to care for me.*

    c.   *They are always very supportive of my decisions*

Student loan debt continues to be a national problem. Talk about your own financial situation as it relates to the misconception that capable low income minority students have their full college costs paid through financial assistance. Have you had to take out student loans because college costs have exceeded your financial aid package?

    a.   *I had a full scholarship, so I did not take out student loans. Book costs were expensive, but definitely manageable.*

b.   *I am mindful of how expensive pre-med programs can be, but have been saving up to pay for that tuition. According to my financial projections, I should have the full amount ($27,000) saved up by September. The schools in my finalized list are all around this price. I do admit that to do this I have had to work full time during summer and winter vacations.*

How diverse was your college experience? Describe the typical student at your college. With whom did you hang out? Were there any special programs offered by the college to help Latino and other minority students cope with the change in cultural context?

a.   *The multicultural scholarship had a great transitional program in which we arrived at the college a couple of days early. We were introduced to other recipients of the scholarship, both in our class and in the upper classes. This was a great way to meet people before the start of classes.*

b.   *We were also paired with upperclassmen who would be our mentors. If we needed help with anything or personal advice they were there for us.*

The college experience is more than what happens in the classroom. What other learning experiences, both in and out of the classroom, have you had that contributed to your growth and development in the past four years?

Recently I started an internship at Orthopedic Associates Inc. This has been an amazing experience. I get to observe doctors in their daily routines, both in office and hospital settings. I am allowed to go into the operating room and observe as they perform surgeries. I have learned a great deal about medicine, patient care, and even health policy.

If I wanted to talk to two professors, administrators, or other educators who know you well and whom you trust and respect, who would they be? How did these people help you?

    a.   *Dr. Levine is my favorite professor at PC. She was my first professor in Health Policy and her enthusiasm for teaching is what drew me into the major. I have loved my experience as a Health Policy student and look forward to using such knowledge to provide better care as a future physician. I have had her for the introductory Health Policy management course, senior seminar, and for a seminar on obesity.*

    b.   *Dr. Hackey is the department chair for the Health Policy program. Here is a professor that truly cares for his student's progress. He does so much extra work to ensure your learning, that it is almost unbelievable. He is always willing to sit down with you if you need help on anything and will read drafts of papers to make sure you hand in your best possible work.*

You are now a college graduate and in front of you are middle school students from Central Falls. They represent a range of abilities from slow learners to honors type students. A large number have struggled academically; some have a sense of hopelessness because of a trail of failure, while others have done well to date. Most are low income Latino students who are facing socio-economic obstacles outside the school. Many have poor school attendance and see little value in school. What do you say to them?

I think words can only go so far. Yes, I would give them advice about hard work, dedication, and seeking help when they need it. However, I think experience is more important. More than just having a conversation, I think physically bringing these students on campus to shadow for a day would be very beneficial. This, I think, would demystify commonly held beliefs about college life, both social and academic. It would also be an opportunity for them to sit in classes that relate to their interests and aspirations.

THIRTEEN

....

GEORGE CARLE

George Carle's college experience is a story of amazing perseverance and resiliency. His journey to date has led many times to frustration and disappointment but, despite that, he has kept his eye on the prize, his dream of getting his college degree and becoming a professional basketball player. His adaptability, focus, and newly found motivation to provide for his newborn son are evidence of his personal growth and maturity. His challenge is best described in James 1:1 *Blessed is the man who perseveres under trial, because when he has stood the test, he will receive the crown of life that God has promised to those who love Him.*

George's responses to the ten questions are much different from those of the other three students who were products of the honors program and shared together many of the same classes and the same outstanding teachers. In many ways, George is more representative of a larger number of Central Falls students who are not as motivated to learn or become "college ready" while in high school. If they are fortunate to attend a technical school, community college or even a four year college after graduation, a high percentage are apt to struggle academically and not complete their degree requirements.

George with his son Jacobb

George's family and personal life are also much different from the other three students. He didn't have the opportunity to attend Central Falls schools for the full twelve years as his family moved frequently and were in and out of Central Falls throughout his formative school years. He was a child of a troubled single mom and had no actual relationship with his biological father whom he saw infrequently. He and his family experienced times when they were homeless and were exposed to a culture of drugs and violence. Although he was considered by Josh LaPlante to be a "smart kid, but developmentally delayed," LaPlante felt George's focus was on athletics and not academics. "He was a confident person on the court but lacked that same confidence in the classroom. Only in his senior year did he realize his academic potential and begin to blossom academically." George also admitted he didn't like to read as a youngster and only when he got to college and experienced some classroom success did he "get turned on to reading."

Although his readiness for college was questionable, George did get accepted into the Talent Development program at the University of Rhode Island (URI) where he could chase his dream to play at the college level and later professional basketball overseas.

George did, however, have two positives going for him. The first was his "likeability." Teachers found him to be kind, humble, and respectful without the attitude of so many high school athletes who act like celebrities as they walk around their school corridors. According to LaPlante, "George was a respected quiet leader who had a clear sense of identity and the potential to be a great leader." His high school basketball coach also confirmed that observation, believing that with continued hard work on his game and in the classroom, George had the potential and athleticism to become a college basketball standout, particularly at a Division II or III college.

The second asset he had was his mother, Rosa Rosado. In 2006, Rosa turned her life around from a previous life that had included drug trafficking and arrests for physical assault. She was fiercely dedicated to her boys and feverishly protected them because she knew of the dangers that lurked in the dark city streets. She didn't want her boys associating with the wrong crowd as she had done. She never abandoned her three sons and kept them on track to get their high school diplomas because she realized that her own lack of education was a major obstacle to getting a well-paying job. Her dream was to have her sons continue their education and achieve their college degrees, particularly her oldest son, George.

George begins his question responses with a long introduction entitled, "A Chronology of the Last Four Long Years." His college journey was indeed a rocky one with its ups and downs, changes in schools, and problems he had to confront at home.

George on the steps of Central Falls High School

He dropped out of the University of Rhode Island after one year because of his poor grades and unsuccessful attempt to be a "walk on" on the basketball team. After taking summer courses at the Community College of Rhode Island (CCRI) and working hard to improve his basketball skills, he enrolled at Lyndon State College in Lyndonville, Vermont, where he planned to play basketball with two former Central Falls basketball classmates.

When he became eligible to play in the second semester at Lyndon, George became discouraged because he received only limited playing time. When he asked his coach why he wasn't playing more, the coach, according to George, told him, "The only reason I don't play you more is because of your bad grades. I don't want to play someone who isn't there all year or maybe the following year." George grew to hate Lyndon and his coach. But his coach was right. George didn't put the effort into his courses as he did in improving his basketball skills and failed several courses that caused him to drop out of Lyndon that spring. His longtime dream of playing college basketball and then playing ball overseas was now shattered. He was miserable.

When George returned to Central Falls, he decided to take a year off and reassess his future. He got a job in a local mill and continued to perfect his basketball skills in local workouts with accomplished players with the hope of returning to college at some point.

During this time, he started dating a friend from high school, Cynthia Cano, who worked as a certified physician's assistant and medical technician in an assisted living facility in Central Falls. Cynthia became pregnant and now life for George became really complicated. The couple decided to have the child and a few months later, a bouncing baby boy, Jacobb, was born, and, yes, he is a big sized handsome fellow who looks exactly like his dad.

George and son Jacobb in front of Central Falls High School

Both his mother Rosa and Cynthia encouraged George to return to Lyndon the following fall to pursue his dream of earning his degree and making a name for himself on the basketball court. Along with Cynthia's mother, they offered to care for the baby while George was away at college. Rosa, in fact, worked the second shift as a press operator making medical devices in a local company in order to take care of Jacobb during the day.

George returned to Lyndon in September, 2013, with a new motivation to succeed and with lasting gratitude to his girlfriend and his mother. According to his mentors and his Lyndon basketball coach, he was now a changed man with a seriousness of purpose and new-found interest in his studies. He regained his academic eligibility with a 3.2 average in his first semester and became a standout as a basketball player. When contacted, his coach said, "George was a mainstay of the team and is one of the better players in the league."

But even with his new-found success, George was torn by not being at home supporting Cynthia and his son. As a father of a newborn son he expresses his despair with these moving words, "It broke my heart, after Jacobb was born, having to leave Cynthia with all the responsibility. It hurt me as a man knowing that I couldn't support my family at this time.

"Looking at my son I see myself. I can't explain how much I love him. My own father was not there for me financially or emotionally, but that is not going to happen to Jacobb. He is my new motivation to make something of myself and completing my college education is an essential part of that mission. Even some of Cynthia's friends questioned her about having me return to college in Vermont as she worked and took care of our new baby. It has not been easy for us."

....

FOURTEEN

GEORGE'S MENTORS

At Central Falls High School several teachers saw George's academic potential and encouraged him to work harder in the classroom. However, it wasn't until his senior year that he applied himself fully to his studies. He expressed his situation this way, "In high school I was a late bloomer and only got real serious about studies in my senior year. My poor literacy skills held me back." Two teachers he respected and who were instrumental in helping him get into college were Josh LaPlante and French teacher Hope Evenoff who was unaware that she had played such a key role in increasing George's self-awareness and confidence as a student.

Hope was a dynamo of a teacher who had been at Central Falls for several years. Her students rated her highly with these kudos: "She rocks. She makes you work hard, but it is worth it." "You know you are learning. It's a tangible thing."

George said similar things about Hope. "She motivated and pushed me to work harder and improve academically." Unfortunately, after the teacher firing debacle, Hope left Central Falls and was quickly hired by a neighboring school district. When contacted she said she wanted a shorter commute from home but in the same breath exclaimed, "But I will always be a Red Warrior!"

Hope had this to say about George: "Quite honestly, I was surprised to be one of the teachers he identified as having helped him, but I did realize his academic potential. I was not initially impressed with him as a student because he never stood out. When he failed a test, I allowed him to retake it and after providing him assistance, he learned quickly. He never complained or got upset about getting poor grades. He knew he could do better and was open to me for assistance. I agree with others; he was kind and respectful and liked by the faculty. Because of his athletic prowess, he was looked up to by other students. He definitely was a good role model for younger students since he didn't have an 'attitude' like some others do."

Unlike the other three students in this book, George did not reach out and maintain contact with his former high school teachers during college. It was not his nature to do so. However, he did stay connected with his high school basketball coach, Brian Crooks, because his dream to play college and professional basketball was always foremost in his mind, outweighing his need to improve in the classroom. That changed dramatically after the birth of his son and he returned to Lyndon with a different set of priorities and made a strong connection with two Lyndon faculty members who helped him immeasurably during his time at Lyndon State.

Angela Ryan-Williams works at Lyndon State College with first generation, low–income students and provides a number of key services for them by finding them tutors and the best financial package, assisting them with course scheduling, or simply listening to their frustrations and helping them resolve issues, whether they be personal or academic.

She had little or no contact with George during his first year at Lyndon but she got to know him well when he returned to campus. She attributes his initial absence in her office to the M.O.

of the male athlete on campus. "They think seeking help is a sign of weakness and an insult to their manhood. But as they become upperclassmen their focus changes and their energy turns to the importance of getting their degree."

She described how her relationship with George changed dramatically after he returned to campus in the fall of 2012. "I noticed a huge difference in him. He was highly motivated and went on to have a great year. He began to work closely with me and my office and that has been an immense help to him. He is forever poking his head in my office to say, 'Hi.' We truly have developed a terrific relationship.

"Let me give you an example of how committed George now is to learning. Knowing I have a young child, he asked me about books he could buy for his son Jacobb for Christmas. George's friends kidded him, reminding him that Jacobb was only a year old! But George was very serious about introducing his son to books early in his life and having his little boy experience the joy of reading. He remembers too well that he never liked to read and the limiting effect that had on him later on. He was going to do all in his power to have his son enjoy reading and be able to read well. It was his responsibility as a father and he accepted it fully."

Angela talked about George and the lack of diversity on campus. "I can understand his initial reaction to lack of diversity at Lyndon, but I feel that has changed for him somewhat with time. We have an increasing number of minority students from Springfield and Albany and our basketball team is now quite diverse. You may know that we have a number of Central Falls' students in the last few years including George's two brothers and his cousin, Rob Alers, who rejoined George on the basketball team this year. George now hangs out with a group of respected basketball friends along with some student friends from the Congo and Sudan."

I asked, "How can George and two brothers afford to go to Lyndon? They don't give athletic scholarships at Division III colleges."

"That's correct. However, George and each of his brothers qualify for $3,000 per year family tuition waiver. When you add federal financial assistance and loans, their cost is more manageable."

"It may be manageable, but still loans are loans and debt that must be paid off."

Angela agreed but explained, "We work very closely with George's mom, Rosa, and all our low income families to get the very best financial package we can get and minimize student debt. And we are very good at that."

When asked what impressed her about George, Angela pretty much underscored the impression given by her colleagues and George's advisor, Professor Anthony Sgherza. "George is a soft spoken, kind hearted young man who truly appreciates the support given him. But don't be fooled; he can be passionate about things, too. He is highly motivated to get his degree and provide for his family. It is more now than just his mother's passion for him to get his college degree. It's now clearly his passion. He will have to work hard but he is capable of getting his degree.

"George also takes personal responsibility for the problems he's had. He doesn't blame his professors or bad luck. He now understands why his coach didn't play him more when he was in academic difficulty. He is determined to take responsibility for his son and do everything he can to provide Jacobb with opportunity for school success and a bright future."

Dr. Sgherza is Department Chair and Professor of Exercise Science and provided valuable feedback on George during a phone interview:

"Anthony, did you give George two D's in the same course?"

"Yes, I did and, believe me, he earned them. In my classes, you have to earn your grade whether it is an A or a D. Knowing that, you might think George and I don't get along, but the opposite is true. I have a great relationship with him. I am a straight talker and George appreciates that. I also find him a fascinating young man.

"I guess we hit it off because of my own background. I grew up in Brooklyn as a white minority kid in a Hispanic neighborhood. As a student, I was successful at failure and cut every corner I could find. I, too, had my share of poor grades. But, like George, when I fell down I kept getting up until I finally changed my act and held myself accountable. That's what George has done. He is now holding himself accountable and working hard in the classroom. And he is getting positive results!

"You need to understand that our courses in exercise science are demanding. It is not an easy program. George is taking such courses as anatomy, chemistry, and physiology. Because our open admissions policy results in enrolling a high number of weak students, as many as one third of the class may drop out of my courses before the end of the semester. Believe me, they are difficult courses and kids have to work hard.

"This semester George is doing well in my anatomy class. He is more highly engaged than ever, especially in our labs where we triple up and have the kids work in a team. He knows enough to team up with some really smart kids, but he's really 'locked in' now and actively contributing to class discussions."

"Dr. Sgherza, explain to me what George will do with his degree in exercise science?"

"Well, exercise science is his major but his specialization is health, fitness, and strength conditioning. He will sit for his credential exam as a personal trainer in his junior year and for his strength conditioning and fitness certification in his senior year.

He also will complete internships and practicums at local hospitals and fitness centers. Given his turnaround academically, I expect George to get his degree and certifications."

"That's great to hear," I said, wondering if George's D grades were coming to an end.

I had a final question. "Earlier you called George a fascinating young man. Could you give me some adjectives to go along with that comment?"

"Well, as I observe him, George is compassionate and very capable. He is what I call a quiet leader. He is like a flower about to blossom."

"That is a real compliment" I countered, "and something I've heard before but not put in such descriptive terms."

As I thanked Anthony for his input he said, "Hopefully we can meet some day." I agreed and told him it would be particularly gratifying if we could meet at George's graduation ceremony in the near future.

....

FIFTEEN

GEORGE'S Q AND A

George adds a preliminary narrative before answering the specific questions asked of the other students. Because of his several changes in colleges and in his personal life, he found it easier to summarize his college journey in the chronology below:

A Chronology of the Last Long Four Years:

I graduated from Central Falls High School in 2009. It was a great accomplishment knowing that both my parents never walked across a graduation stage, although they eventually got their GED.

Being a leader on my high school basketball team, I dreamed of becoming a professional basketball player in the NBA or at least play overseas. With that in mind, I went to the University of Rhode Island (URI) and tried to walk on and become a member of their Division I basketball team. Unfortunately, the coach had a full roster of scholarship players and there was no room for a walk-on like me. However, I wasn't discouraged and continued to work on my game and improve. Eventually, I caught the eye of the team's best player and was invited to the team's personal workouts and practices and did well enough to realize I could improve and be a strong college player somewhere.

I knew it would be a long time before I would get a chance to show URI my "stuff." I knew I would get better because I was confident, I had what it took, but I couldn't wait. Only a freshman, I could transfer to another smaller college where I would have a chance of play right away.

But a problem occurred. Because I continued to work so hard on improving my game, I was slacking off on my academics and my GPA took a nose dive. This hurt because Salve Regina College in Newport was heavily recruiting me , allowing me to stay close to home and play ball. Unfortunately, my academic problems denied me that opportunity.

So I dropped out of URI, took some summer courses at the Community College of Rhode Island (CCRI) and was offered an opportunity to play basketball and pursue my degree at Lyndon State College in Vermont. Why Vermont, cold snowy Vermont? It was simple. First, my cousin and close friend were at Lyndon and were playing basketball there. Secondly, I needed a change of scenery. I needed to get away and start somewhere fresh. I noticed that a lot of my friends never realized their dreams because they stayed in Central Falls and Pawtucket and didn't reach out and seek opportunity elsewhere. There was nothing here for me in Rhode Island so I left for Vermont of all places.

In Vermont it was difficult for me to fit in. They are country people and I'm a city kid. I love the city. It took me a long while to get used to the northern Vermont culture and environment.

I easily made the basketball team but had a frustrating and disappointing season. I had to wait for my chance to play after everyone else, especially the seniors on the team who lacked the talent I did, but got more playing time. I was capable of being a starter but wasn't and it was driving me crazy. There were times I cried because I knew what I could do but didn't get a real chance. In the meantime, my grades were not good. The coach pulled me aside and told me the only reason he didn't play me more was because of my poor grades. He did not want to play someone who wasn't going to be there all year or maybe not the following year.

My grades did improve somewhat but I failed a key class second semester and was ready to quit everything because I became athletically ineligible. Quite simply, I hated the coach and I hated Vermont. I decided to take a year off and reassess my future.

So I came home to Central Falls and became involved with a young lady and high school friend, Cynthia Cano. Cynthia helped me immensely to get over my lost year in Vermont. Taking the year off was a huge decision but I knew I needed to get my head right for school and my goal of playing college basketball. I worked locally, went to CCRI and took some courses. Then I learned that Cynthia was pregnant.

Although the thought of being a father was exciting, it was also scary. Cynthia and I decided to go through with the pregnancy and had a very healthy son, Jacobb George Carle. My mother, Rosa Rosado, stepped forward to help us with the new baby. I can't tell you what deep gratitude I have for those two amazing women.

It was now time for me to get serious about my future. I had a new determination unlike ever before. I had to get back to college, regain my eligibility to play basketball, and get my college degree. I needed to keep my dream alive while at the same time assume my responsibility as the father of my child.

My own father was not there for me financially or emotionally but this was not going to happen to Jacobb. He was my new motivation to make something of myself and completing my college education was an essential part of that mission.

I therefore went back to Lyndon in the fall of 2012 and had a successful semester academically achieving a 3.2 grade point average. I regained my eligibility in second semester and started at small forward where I averaged 12 points and 7 rebounds a game. My opportunity to make a name for myself as a basketball player and attain my degree by completing four more semesters was alive and well. Maybe playing professional basketball overseas was not just a pipe dream after all.

How have you changed as a person because of your college experience?

I grew up in the last four years, mentally and physically. I have a clearer purpose in my life. I was a mediocre student who didn't like to read and spent too much time having fun with his friends to someone who now actually enjoys his courses and "hitting the books."

I was a decent basketball player who has improved to the point of now being a mainstay and leader on my college team and starting to establish a reputation throughout Vermont.

Reflect on your college experience. Rate it on a scale from 1 to 10 (10 being the highest). What have been some of the highlights and lowlights?

My college experience has been a mixture of the good and the bad. It is not fun to be behind academically and work as hard as I did to regain my basketball eligibility and not be on the verge of dismissal from school. Adapting to a new school environment in Vermont was a challenge as well. But with the birth of my son it has opened my eyes to why I went back to school. It is for my son and my future. It is more than my success; it is now for my family's success as well. My ranking for my Lyndon State experience has risen to a 7 out of 10 after a sluggish and frustrating start.

You have told me that parents, brothers, sisters, past teachers, etc., have played an important role in your college success. What are some illustrations of the special support and encouragement they gave you?

My mother helped me emotionally and financially. It was not her responsibility but she stepped forward and helped Cynthia with Jacobb when I went back to college.

Cynthia, my girlfriend, was with me throughout keeping my head straight and enabling me to return to college. She is a strong woman who swallowed her pride and supported me and my son this past year. I couldn't have asked for any more from her; she is a good friend, a good person, and a great mother to Jacobb.

At first it was hard to realize that I was a parent of a newborn. It finally hit me after we took the baby home from the hospital and then waking up at 3 a.m. that reality set in. Looking at Jacobb, I saw myself. I can't explain how much I love him. It broke my heart to leave him after he was born, leaving Cynthia with all the responsibility. It hurt me as a man knowing I could not support my family at that time. Some of Cynthia's friends even questioned her about having me return to college in Vermont as she worked and took care of our new baby. It was not easy for us to do, but we did it.

Student loan debt continues to be a national problem. Talk about your own financial situation as it relates to the misconception that capable low income minority students have their full college costs paid through financial assistance. Have you had to take out student loans because college costs have exceeded your financial aid package?

I expect to pay off my loans after I graduate; hopefully, after I sign a contract to play basketball overseas. With my degree in athletic training I expect to take care of my college debt while at the same time supporting my son and his mother whether I am playing basketball or not.

If I wanted to talk to two professors, administrators, or other educators who know you well and whom you trust and respect, who would they be? How did these people help you?

Two people at Lyndon I respect and who helped me the most were Angela Ryan-Williams and Professor Sqherza. Sqherza, a professor in exercise science, was always tough on me and twice gave me a D in the same class! But he never gave up on me! He was always pushing me to the next level. I respect him for that because it motivated me to return to school and realize I could do well in the classroom if I really applied myself.

Angie works in student services with low income, first generation students and has been an immense help to me both academically and personally. Both of these people have guided me in the right direction and have contributed to my success after I reentered Lyndon in the fall of 2012.

You are now a college graduate and in front of you are middle school students from Central Falls. They represent a range of abilities from slow learners to honors type students. A large number have struggled academically; some have a sense of hopelessness because of a trail of failure, while others have done well to date. Most are low income Latino students who are facing socio-economic obstacles outside the school. Many have poor attendance and see little value in school. What do you say to them?

I would say make the best of all your opportunities in school now. Go the extra mile and understand the importance of getting good grades. I have been there and done all the fun and popular things, but in the end those things don't matter. School success should be a priority, not fun. I wish I could go back in time and take school more seriously than I did. It would have avoided much pain and frustration along the up and down journey I have been on during the last four years.

SIXTEEN

....

TWO SPECIAL TEACHERS

What does it take to achieve success as a teacher in an inner city high school where poverty is a major obstacle to learning? There are excellent and competent teachers in every school, whether urban, suburban, or rural, who are fully dedicated to their students. However, are there certain essential and unique skills, qualities, and understandings inner city teachers must have as they find themselves teaching to large numbers of students with low expectations, many of them facing adversity almost every day of their young lives?

Recently I met a former college classmate in Wal-Mart whom I hadn't seen for over fifty years. As we stood at the store's entrance sharing our life experiences, I learned that she had retired three years earlier after having spent her entire career teaching low income minority children in an inner city school in Philadelphia. I listened intently as she shared her thoughts with me, "If you love your students there is no job more rewarding than teaching inner city kids. And I loved my students. Unfortunately, I saw too many teachers with low expectations for our students and whose body language reflected that negative thinking, and that distressed me."

Her words stuck with me for the rest of the day and long thereafter. She was saying, "Love is having high expectations and never, never, giving up on your students." I thought of a myriad of other phrases I have used in the past to describe high quality teachers; however, the most important were definitely those simple words used by my classmate. All the other teacher characteristics and qualifications one could list mean nothing without first having teachers love their students and hold high expectations for them. If this happens, what follows is that they then love their job in spite of the frustrations and challenges that confront them.

Whenever I reflect on our chance meeting, I will always remember the forceful passion in my classmate's voice and the serious expression on her face. She obviously had worked hard at her craft and now looks back with fondness and gratitude for the opportunity she had had to change children's lives. She considers it a special gift that has enriched her life.

My classmate's comments reminded me of the teachers I have met and come to know in Central Falls High School who have high standards and expectations for their students, a passion for their subject, and are skilled in building student relationships that are based upon mutual respect and caring. Students find these teachers genuine and realize that they have to work hard and give a full effort in their classes.

Without doubt, teaching in an inner city classroom is very challenging when a large number of students are low achievers with academic deficits caused by poor school attendance and other socio-economic factors. As a result, many have brought with them a record of failure and feelings of hopelessness. Granted, there are students like this in suburban classrooms as well; however, there are considerably more students in this category in Central Falls High School. There is, therefore, a need for creative, inspiring, and knowledgeable teachers in inner city classrooms, teachers whom students respect and trust.

Despite its problems and its bad press, Central Falls High School has always been fortunate to have had some excellent teachers who were able to draw exciting results from their students. Doris White and Deloris Grant are two of those teachers. Both taught and mentored students featured in this book. Doris is an art teacher who offers a range of elective courses to the entire student body. Deloris teaches English to both honors and regular, as well as inclusion classes. Both teachers were born and raised in Central Falls and embody those qualities which allow them to motivate their students and have them achieve at their highest level. Both are veteran teachers having taught at the high school for their entire careers.

Doris White

If you walk pass Doris White's art classroom on the ground floor of the high school while students are moving to their next class, you will notice that Doris has locked her door. Students stand outside the door waiting to enter. This happens for each class, every day

On the day of my visit, the students are looking up at a typed message above the door which contains the thought for the day, and that is why she locks her door. She wants them to read, think, and talk about the daily message before they enter the classroom. Today it is a quote from Maya Angelou: "People will forget what you said, but they will never forget how you made them feel." Doris suddenly appears and opens the door and the students head for their assigned tables. Doris starts the class immediately by asking her class to react to the quotation. Her skill in facilitating class discussion and helping students to think is obvious. She has honed her technique over the eighteen years she has been teaching at the high school.

Her art room is bright and cheery with colorful exhibits of student work. There is no clutter in this art room and students know where to get the tools they need to continue their assignments in her 3D design class. Students are making a sarcophagus that will be glazed and submitted along with a completed written rubric analysis indicating that that they have met the eighteen stated course outcomes. Printed articles on Egyptian culture, especially on Egyptian burial traditions, are the source of class discussions since Doris believes strongly in an interdisciplinary integrated approach to teaching art.

On one of the walls in her classroom is a large sign that reads, "To Be a Teacher is My Greatest Piece of Work." As she moves nimbly from table to table helping students with their projects, her outgoing personality, warm smile, and exuberance all speak to the love she has for her students and her subject. There is "no fooling around" in the organized laboratory environment she has created in the lowest level of this 1928 school building. Students are serious as they concentrate on etching 3000 BC hieroglyphic inscriptions on each side of their sarcophagus.

When asked the secret to her success in motivating students and gaining their respect, she had a ready answer: "Teaching is being able to build a relationship and knowing how to walk and talk with inner city kids. I share with them who I am and where I came from. I tell them I wasn't born with a silver spoon in my mouth and I grew up in Central Falls where my family and I went through some tough times. Education wasn't valued either. I learned the hard way with taking a series of low paying jobs and realizing that, without further education, I would never get anywhere. Because I now had a family of my own, it took me ten years to get my degree and certification. I began teaching in Central Falls in 1995 and was able to identify with my students and earn their respect. I care about them and they know it. I particularly enjoy following them and their paths after graduation."

One of those students she remained connected with was Bryant Estrada who called Doris, "One of the most influential teachers in my life and a positive role model who, during the teacher firings, stayed strong and didn't move a muscle." They met for lunch periodically during his college years and continue to do so. Doris was there for Bryant during his freshman year academic struggles and later with his amazing turnaround and recently, during his ambivalence about becoming a medical doctor. He solicits her advice and appreciates her honesty. He credits Doris with discovering his love for visual art when he took two of her ceramics courses. Doris explains his transformation as follows: "When Bryant entered my Ceramics II class I watched him grow and mature and he began to develop his technical and creative skills. In his senior year when he took Advanced Ceramics, his work began to explode with expression, technique, critical thinking, and problem-solving skills. The experience allowed him to 'de-stress' and forget about life's pressures." The exposure to art that she gave Bryant surely served him well at Brown when things looked bleak. It was his outlet and helped him survive academically.

After almost two decades of teaching, Doris stays connected with many of her former students and takes pride in their achievements. She is still discovering and developing the hidden creative talents of her students and teaching them to study and appreciate art, not solely for its intrinsic value but also for the acquisition of skills that are important in academic and life success. Her creed, "To Be a Teacher is My Greatest Piece of Work," remains deeply imbedded in her heart and mind and, like Bryant, her students know this and, as a result, respond positively to her love and concern for them.

Deloris Grant

Deloris Grant is an exceptional English and drama teacher. Just ask her students. Recently, students in both honors and inclusive English classes shared their thoughts on Deloris. "She makes it interesting," shared one student, while another said, "She is hard and gives a lot of work but I learned a lot." My favorite response was, "She is a creative teacher with a heart" because it highlights Deloris' deep desire to see her students succeed. She is highly animated with a charismatic personality that fully engages her students. Her enthusiasm, excitement, and passion for her work are a true gift to her students. She works hard at her craft and expects her students to work just as hard as she does. Teaching the text is only the beginning of the process for Deloris; she also focuses on critical thinking skills and the joy of literature and language, a joy that she hopes stays with her students long after they leave her classroom.

Deloris, like Doris White, grew up in Central Falls and graduated from Central Falls High School. She said, "My family was dirt poor and at the time was the only black family in the city. Although my parents never went beyond eighth grade, they made sure that my four sisters and I attended school every day. No excuses. We also had plenty of books at home that our parents encouraged us to read."

Deloris admits that she did not get serious about going to college until two teachers encouraged her to take advanced courses and convinced her that going to a good college was well within her reach. Now Deloris is returning that favor by working tirelessly to help her students succeed and reach their full potential.

Deloris taught honors English to Bryant, Theresa, and Guillermo and their tributes to her appear in earlier chapters of this book. Along with Doris White, Bryant considers Deloris a superb teacher and another role model. Guillermo credits her as a being part of his "school family" and someone who contributed greatly to his social development and academic success. Theresa considers Deloris a trusted friend and mentor who has supported and encouraged her at every turn.

Deloris stays connected with all three of them and is proud of their college success. A woman with strong feelings about education, she gets upset when people imply that the Central Falls' high school curriculum has been "dumbed down." "I take offense when I am told that our teachers teach to the minimum just because we are educators at an urban school. I introduce my students to many college texts and practice high level, demanding writing and speaking and that is why Bryant, Theresa, and Guillermo were prepared for college level work. I will not take all the honors. They came with willing hearts and minds to learn, as well as a respect for learning."

Deloris believes that making connections with students and listening to who they are is the first step to the student respecting you as a teacher. She sees respect as a two way street. "Students respect me because I don't lie. Sometimes they need to hear the hard truths. I share a common background with them and they tend to trust me when they find out who I am. There are few students I can't reach. The ones that slip through never attend school to give me a chance."

Deloris also possesses another essential quality of a good teacher and that is the desire and drive to keep improving her skills. She understands that even if you are successful, you should always be trying to get better and grow professionally, especially in this age of new and improved instructional strategies and technological breakthroughs. She mentions a series of professional activities and associations that have kept her on the cutting edge in her field. "I love the ability to be creative and the room to grow my creativity. I have edited three adapted versions of Shakespeare's plays for my drama and English classes that are now used in other high schools. I am now an author!

"I am also part of the new urban education collaboration with Rhode Island College (RIC) where we are preparing student teachers to teach in an urban setting. This year I was assigned my first student teacher since the firing. She was amazing. I had forgotten how much I love teaching teachers. What was even more revealing is that many of the RIC professors observed my classes and were in disbelief that my students were so disciplined and able to read and comprehend Shakespeare and had the ability to do Socratic seminars. They, along with the general public, really believed that we were incompetent, lazy, and lacked the ability to teach."

Shared Philosophies

Although interviewed separately, it was telling that Deloris and Doris shared similar philosophies about teaching disadvantaged inner city kids. Both believe that respect between teacher and student is vitally important to their effectiveness as teachers. This acknowledgement is nothing new; in fact, Deloris and Doris echo a belief held by Ralph Waldo Emerson who said, "The most important thing a teacher must have is respect for the student." The challenge, however, is for teachers to know how to give that respect before they can receive it from their students. Deloris and Doris know how to make their students feel worthwhile and convince them that they can overcome the barriers that are in their way. That means hard work, especially in encouraging students to believe in themselves and to stay motivated. Teachers like Deloris and Doris must encourage their students to aim high. They must remind them that they do not have to be in honors classes to be a success in life. They must assure them that they have the potential within them to work hard and achieve. Above all, they must model sacrifice, discipline, personal pride, and staying the course. The most important thing disadvantaged inner city youth need is teachers and mentors who, at key points in their lives, make them believe in themselves. When teachers like Deloris and Doris believe in them that can make all the difference.

SEVENTEEN

....

SUMMARY AND CONCLUSIONS

In writing this book I had two major goals. First, I wanted to learn what challenges and obstacles four Central Falls graduates faced in college having graduated from an urban high school classified by the media and educational officials as a "drop out factory." The second goal was to determine how well they were prepared for college work by their high school teachers.

As revealed in the book, there were many challenges. Three of the four students did get their degrees. George Carle needs to complete a shade less than two years of courses in order to get his degree. He still has several academic barriers to hurdle if he is to attain his degree in exercise science.

Financial Challenges

George, along with Bryant and Theresa, had to assume college loans in spite of the financial assistance provided by their colleges. With two other brothers also in college and his mother temporarily unemployed, money was scarce, especially after his son was born.

Bryant took a leave of absence from his post bachelor health studies at the University of Pennsylvania in January, 2014, when he realized that financing his pursuit to become a medical doctor

119

would be a serious financial burden to his family and himself. Coupled with his ambivalence about wanting to become a physician, he felt a need to explore other career options while at the same time working and saving money.

George, Theresa, and Bryant sitting on the school steps
Motto, "Dream Big, Dream Fierce"

Theresa, although on scholarship, wanted the full college experience and that meant living on campus. As a result, she had to assume student loans and rely on her sister to support her other learning experiences off campus, such as overseas travel and attendance at national conferences. Because of the need to provide financial support for her mother, she sought employment close to home and postponed her ambition to live and work on the West Coast.

On the other hand, Guillermo has yet to take out a student loan. His honors scholarship at Providence College and money he saved from part time work covered his tuition and fees. The fact that he also commuted to school for four years and lived at home allowed him to accumulate enough money to pay for the post bachelor health program at Northeastern, which he will begin next fall. Money was, however, a factor in his decision to go to Northeastern. With his credentials, he could have gone to Columbia, which was his first choice. Following a lengthy discussion with his parents, he chose Northeastern because it was a better financial fit. Guillermo also realizes that it is just a matter of time before he will need to take out loans. It is inevitable. "Medical school is much more expensive, so I definitely will need to take out loans at that time," he explains.

Cultural Diversity

Adjusting to the social environment was also a challenge, since the four students graduated from a high school that was nearly seventy percent Latino. With the exception of Brown, a lack of cultural diversity was evident at Roger Williams, Lyndon State, and Providence College. At Brown, the Third World Center (TWC) served as Bryant's oasis and home, a comforting place that helped him survive in his freshman year and adapt to an entirely new social and academic environment. The TWC was his springboard to academic success and a leadership/mentor role where he helped other minority students adapt to Brown's unique culture and achieve success as he did.

Guillermo commuted and spent less time on campus except for playing intramural soccer where he seriously injured his knee and lost a semester from school. He took advantage of a multicultural scholarship transitional program where he interacted with other minority honors scholarship students and later was assigned upperclassmen who served as his student mentors.

Lyndon State had few minority students on campus although, like other colleges, it was committed to recruiting more students of color and providing the support services needed. As he recounted, it was a culture shock to George, a city kid in the hills of Vermont with few minorities other than a handful of athletes and international students. George was lucky, however, because he befriended academic advisors who connected with him, realized his potential, and guided him through rocky waters, both social and academic.

Theresa had a similar experience at Roger Williams, which she found to be a school "mainly of white students with a lot of money." She did admit that the school was proactive in trying to recruit students from urban school districts and not appear as an institution where a degree was financially unattainable to capable minority students with limited resources. However, during her time there she said, "Anyone who says RWU (Roger Williams University) is diverse is, unfortunately, . . . lying. It really isn't." Although culturally shocked when she arrived on campus, she adapted admirably by turning a negative into a positive.

What she said is worth repeating, ". . . life is about learning and embracing your environment. Just because the campus wasn't the diverse crowd I was used to, didn't mean I had a bad time. In fact, I had a great experience there. I did establish friendships with people of different ethnicities because we all had similar interests, but they weren't the only people I hung out with."

The Importance of Mentors

All four students felt their college experience was very positive and that it had a profound effect on them, providing them with increased confidence, self-understanding, and independence. According to Bryant, "I have become more socially conscious, mature, and have learned to solidify my opinions and articulate them well."

The fact that the students did well in college can be attributed to a number of things, but the most important factor was the mentoring and support they received on and off campus. They were not hesitant to seek support, assistance, and counsel from professors, academic advisors, former high school teachers and members of their family. For example, Theresa's public relations professor, Dr. Aimee Shelton, opened multiple doors for Theresa and engaged her in professional and personal growth activities off campus. Working closely with Dr. Robert Hackey, Guillermo constantly expanded his knowledge base and improved the quality of his work.

Although George's personality made him reluctant at first to ask for help, his academic support advisor, Angela Ryan-Williams, became his friend and mentor and provided him with the support and direction he critically needed.

High school teachers like Doris White, Ron Thompson, and Deloris Grant stayed connected to their former students and played key roles as mentors. Bryant's and Guillermo's parents, Theresa's sister Amanda, George's mother Rosa and his girlfriend Cynthia were all instrumental in the students' success in college. The sacrifices and support of these people cannot be underrated. If students who face major obstacles are to succeed, it is imperative that they have people around them on whom they can lean and to whom they can go for guidance, support, and even comfort. Having such caring people in their lives that they trusted and respected made all the difference for Bryant, Theresa, Guillermo and George.

Challenging Curriculum

Bryant, Theresa, and Guillermo did well in college. In fact, it was more than just doing well; they excelled. They are living proof that the honors curriculum at Central Falls High School was not "watered down." It was a demanding program involving teachers who understood urban learners and taught critical thinking skills as well as basic skills. They knew how to teach to their willing students without having to "dumb down" the curriculum.

When discussing this issue with several teachers, they admitted that some of their colleagues need to improve. At the same time, they caution critics to understand that teachers should not be held accountable for the poverty that exists, especially when it causes students to miss a large number of school days during the course of a year. They feel that urban teachers have to educate themselves on how to best educate disadvantaged inner city students and this means specialized teacher training in urban classrooms with experienced and skillful teacher mentors.

Deloris Grant reports that many pedagogical methods used by urban teachers simply do not work. Many teachers overuse direction and insistence on student compliance. This can provoke student resentment, and sometimes, actual resistance. Teachers experience burnout, expending emotional energy to maintain their authority. Deloris contends that students do not want to be controlled. She said, "Bryant, Theresa, and Guillermo do not fit the mold of undisciplined students. They chose to take demanding classes being taught by educators who understand effective educational practice."

It is, therefore, not surprising that the three Central Falls honors program students excelled in college ahead of classmates from honors programs in other public and private high schools. Clearly this would not have happened if they had been products of a "watered down" curriculum.

Questions Raised

Several key questions emerge when learning of the incredible success of the honors students in college: Are the best teachers in the school teaching in the honors program? What about the students in the rest of the school: are they being shortchanged? Do any of the experienced, highly successful honors teachers teach classes other than honors classes? These are fair questions, which deserve honest answers.

In talking with several honors teachers, I learned that most of them do have mixed schedules teaching honors, inclusion, and regular education classes. As an art teacher, Doris offers classes to all students. Her challenge is to encourage students to take more advanced art courses, something she convinced Bryant to do.

Deloris teaches English to other than just honors students and has done so for a long time. She e-mailed me this response to my questions, which obviously had struck a chord with her: "I have continued to teach inclusion English and I am proud of my successes, if success means graduation. I keep close connections with all my former students. I do not distinguish my relationship with students as advanced placement, honors, inclusion, or regular education. They are young minds waiting on the doorstep of life. It is my job to help them communicate ideas. I have former students who are doctors, lawyers, teachers, musicians, artists, designers, in jail, unemployed. I had a student recently whom I inducted into the International Thespian Society. He advanced from my inclusion class to my advanced placement class. He is now a Marine. I have never been prouder."

Another important question needs to be addressed. Are the three honors students really representative of the majority of Central Falls students? The short answer is, "No; they are the exception."

However, George Carle does represent a large percentage of the school population that has grown up with residential instability, and other domestic challenges. George experienced homelessness, exposure to the drug culture, and the dire effects of poverty. His mother Rosa had her brushes with the law and found herself having to raise three boys by herself. Not until 2006 when George was in high school did she turn herself around and escape from a lifestyle of crime and drugs.

George did have several things going for him. The first was a dream that generally is an unrealistic one held by many urban youth: a dream to play professional basketball. In George's case, his dream is still alive and has kept him in pursuit of his college degree. At the same time, it has become so much of a priority that it has negatively affected his academic progress after flashes of his academic potential had impressed both his high school and college teachers.

The second factor that has kept George on a path to obtain his high school diploma and college degree was the three women who believed in him. The first was his mother Rosa, who, in spite of her own troubles, was fiercely devoted to her three sons and kept them on straight paths, insisting they not make the life mistakes that she had made. She protected them with a passion by setting curfews, insisting homework be completed, monitoring their friends, and demanding they do everything in their power to obtain their high school diplomas and go on to college. Then there was Cynthia, his girlfriend, who financially supported him and encouraged him to return to college after their son was born. And finally there was George's academic counselor and friend at Lyndon State College, Angela Ryan-Williams, who was instrumental in George's successful return to college.

George, therefore, may best be described as an intelligent young man whose learning and basic skill development were delayed in his early school years and who, as a result, has been a marginal student, especially in college. He is more representative of the center of the Central Falls student body with the honors students being at one end and high risk, failing students at the other end. He is a student whose academic potential was not fully realized due to the circumstances of his early life. Unfortunately, too many of George's classmates fall into this category and need special assistance and trusting mentors as they navigate the waters of higher education.

Where Are They Now?

It has been nearly a year since Bryant, Theresa, and Guillermo graduated with distinction from college. George has completed slightly more than two years' worth of credits toward his degree in exercise science, having met his general education requirements and passed several of his required science courses. Here is a breakdown of where the four students are at the moment.

Guillermo, Bryant, Theresa, George and Jacobb at Central Falls High School

Bryant Estrada

Bryant has ended his leave and permanently left the post-baccalaureate pre-health program at the University of Pennsylvania and is moving in another career direction. He enjoys teaching and has been a busy substitute teacher in a number of school districts in the Providence area. His past experience of teaching math to ninth and tenth graders in the College Crusade Saturday program was most rewarding and sparked his interest in pursuing a graduate degree in education and getting a teaching position in a charter school. As is his style, Bryant is weighing his future options with great deliberation and seeking the sage advice of his mentors.

Guillermo Ronquillo

Because his knee surgery caused him to lose a semester, Guillermo graduated in January, 2014, and has been working and saving his money since that time to pay the costs of his post-baccalaureate pre-medical health program at Northeastern University for the 2014-2015 school year. Guillermo works for his dad's company cleaning office buildings and plowing snow in the bad weather. When asked if he makes big money, he responded, "I wish." But knowing Guillermo, the money he makes goes into the bank to support his dream of becoming a medical doctor.

Theresa Agonia

Theresa was fortunate to work for the Latino Institute at Roger Williams University immediately upon graduation for a few months with responsibility for internal and external communications before taking a position as Business Outreach and Public Relations Coordinator for the city of Central Falls. She is a member of Mayor James Diossa's leadership team and does event planning and handles all communications for the city. Interestingly, the twenty-eight-year-old Diossa is a Central Falls graduate who, like Theresa, shares a passion for the city and is taking positive steps to return it to prominence after the period of state receivership. Theresa loves her job and reports, "I feel so fortunate to work in my home town and be able to give back to my community."

The city of Central Falls is also fortunate to have a woman with the talents of Theresa working for its improvement.

George Carle

George's situation is a bit more complex than the other students. His responsibilities at home weighed heavily on him as his son Jacobb had some developmental language issues that eventually were seen as normal delay by the family's doctors. While in Vermont, he really missed his young son and his girlfriend Cynthia and wanted to be with them and assume his responsibilities as a dad.

George did have a challenging second semester at Lyndon State with some demanding science courses that he eventually failed. After weighing his options, George decided to take on-line courses in the summer and return to Lyndon in the fall to complete his degree requirements and play basketball since he had one year of eligibility left. It was not an easy decision for George to make because it postponed his plan to play professional basketball overseas and again meant separation from his son and girlfriend. But he realized it was his best option, especially if he could do his required internship in the Providence area rather than in Vermont. His son was also doing well and this was of great relief to him.

Recent reports indicate that George did well in his on-line courses, regained his eligibility, and is back at Lyndon for the fall 2014 semester, where he expects to continue to pursue his degree and play a major leadership role on the basketball team.

George, back in action on the court

Final Thoughts

Years from now, you may wonder what might happen to the four students profiled in this book. Will their dreams be fulfilled?

Will Bryant be voted state math teacher of the year and appointed head of his own charter school? Will Guillermo be a noted orthopedic surgeon? Will Theresa be a director and owner of her own public relations company? Will George actually play professional basketball overseas and complete his degree requirements, and eventually become a successful personal trainer in a major fitness facility?

One thing is for sure: I won't bet against them.

APPENDIX 1

....

GUILLERMO'S COLLEGE ESSAY (2009)

I Am a Survivor

I believe that some human beings are born with a certain competitive edge that nature has proven vital for survival. When in the face of defeat, this competitive nature removes all that is base in our beings, and brings out what is necessary to achieve victory in our everyday struggles. In my life, it is not a battle or a struggle for survival in nature which brings out the best in me, but rather a struggle for success. Furthermore, it is this competitive nature that allows me to fight and overcome all that stands in my way.

So what happens to those who choose to give up rather than pursue their goals? I suppose they are merely too afraid of failure to even try to be successful. I do not believe that a person is a coward if they feel fear, but once that person allows fear to overcome their sense of duty, they become one. My duty is to my God and to my family first. They have always protected and supported me. My duty is to love them and to honor them in everything I do.

Secondly, I have a duty to one day be happy and successful. In every step of my life I have never let go of that sense of duty. That is why every night before I go to bed and every morning before I go to school, I kneel down before my God and ask him for his guidance and for strength. My dreams and goals are driven by that very sense of duty, and my competi-

tive nature compels me to do the best that I can do. These two qualities, duty and competitiveness, are deep within my character, and they only grow stronger as I overcome obstacles in my daily life.

At the age of nine, my move from El Salvador to the United States presented a series of challenges. There was a stark contrast between my academic abilities in the two countries. Not only did I confront a significant communication barrier due to my limited English skills, but also the system of education to which I was subjected left me confused. Nevertheless, my competitive nature and developing motivation to surmount obstacles met these challenges head on. Ironically, it was the drastic change in grades and proficiency that has compelled me to reach the top of my high school class today.

During my first year in the ESL class, my teacher was trying to explain to me how in English, as opposed to Spanish, an adjective can come before a noun. When she saw that I was having a hard time, she got up to leave and said, "stupid kid" under her breath. Though I didn't speak English, I knew exactly what she had said. The single incident awoke my competitive nature and made me work harder. One year later, I was moved into mainstream English classes. Because of my inherent desire to advance and the support I found in other teachers, I was able to adapt.

I learned two valuable things from my move to the United States. One is that, though there will always be naysayers, there are even more people who believe in me. In the face of defeat, they plant enough hope in my mind and heart to keep me moving forward. Secondly, I learned that, while my environment changed completely, this country has provided fertile ground for me to grow as a better person, a hardworking person, and ultimately, a success.

Charles Darwin said that the organism that is most likely to survive is that which is capable of adapting to a new environment. This notion not only applies to the scientific world, but also in the human race towards success. The environments in which we live, work, and study will change. The survivors are those who learn to adapt. In my academic career, after *adopting a new culture, I learned to adapt as the social and educational conditions changed. These conditions change for all students as they move on to each subsequent grade level.*

Some will give up, while others, the survivors, will advance. I am a survivor. My past experiences have proven so. Moving on to college, and later on to medical school, the challenges will only heighten. Whether it is trying to find a way to pay for college tuition, or struggling through an exam, I know the path I have chosen is not an easy one. Even so, driven by my competitiveness and my duties, and keeping my faith in God, I will be successful. For those who believe in me, I will work hard. In the face of naysayers, I will work even harder to prove them wrong.

....

GUILLERMO'S ESSAY TO GRADUATE SCHOOL (2014)

Why Do You Want to Prepare for a Career in a Medical Field?

There were five minutes left in the game. The score was 4-3 and my team was on the losing end. Tired but unwilling to lose, the referee's kick-off whistle pushed us forward on our last breath. As I jumped for a header near the goal, I felt a shove from behind and heard a loud snap in my right leg. The pain was piercing, almost unbearable, but the news of a torn ACL would be devastating.

From a young age I fell in love with soccer and its strategic approach to fast-paced competition, the teamwork necessary to play effectively, and the seemingly inherent passion of "the beautiful game." Whether playing a weekend match with friends, competing in a regional tournament, or thinking through a major life decision, alone on the green pitch with a wide open net, soccer had always been an important part of my life. Yet this new injury threatened to take away my ability to play regularly and competitively. Were it not for medical innovation and the development of ACL reconstruction surgery, I would no longer be able to enjoy playing the sport today.

Certainly, going through the treatment and rehabilitation process for an ACL injury introduced me to orthopedics and inspired me to prepare for a career in the field. As a patient, I saw firsthand how both my doctors and physical therapists were empathetic to my needs, provided me with compassionate care, and, perhaps most importantly, practiced evidence based medicine to ensure my safe return to athletic activity. Indeed, going into my undergraduate education as a health policy and management major I knew I wanted to enter a profession that would involve service to others, and this experience introduced me to a field where altruism, athletics, and cutting-edge science all come together to prevent, treat, and rehabilitate musculoskeletal ailments.

My academic internship experience at Orthopedic Associates, Inc. my senior year of college further reinforced my decision to pursue a career in medicine. During my time there I saw cases that went beyond athletic-related injuries. I was able to shadow both doctors and physical therapists during regular office visits and surgeries for a variety of common orthopedic conditions. Moreover, while most of the patients I met were not athletes and many of their conditions were described as "routine" by the physicians, the underlying responsibility to provide compassionate care and choose a treatment option that would best reduce pain and return normal bodily function to each individual patient kept me coming back every week of the semester.

Most notably, I learned how important it is for the provider to establish a relationship where the patient shares in the decision-making process and where the doctor takes on the role of the trusted professional guiding the patient through that decision. As a future physician I would like to exhibit this kind of empathy and patient-centered care. I believe that establishing trust with patients and involving them in the decision-making process makes for meaningful conversations, increases the likelihood of patients following through with all aspects of established treatments, and increases the overall quality of care. I learned that being a good physician doesn't just men having a sophisticated understanding of medical science, but also maintaining humility in the practice of medicine. That is, always remembering that medicine entails one person attempting to understand and help another.

....

BRYANT'S COLLEGE ESSAY (2009)

Monopoly: Surreal Becoming Reality

I went down to the basement to help my mother clean out some old stuff: she said that the cleaning was "a time to throw away the useless junk that had been building up for years." I searched through my childhood toys, different things that I had not seen for years. A Monopoly box was at the bottom of the pile; it was a game that I had not seen or played since I was ten, when I would wake up on Saturdays at seven o'clock in the morning to watch cartoons and play with my older sister. As I opened the dusty box, many childhood memories came running through my head. The game board fell to the floor and it opened. I rolled the dice; the game had begun.

The board began to tremble on the ground. Everything disappeared and the world around me seemed to turn back. A sudden light began to envelop my surroundings, and I noticed I was no longer in the basement with my childhood memorabilia. Everything looked very similar, as if I had seen it all before, I was on the game board! Two dice fell onto the floor and my body unwillingly began to move. It was as if the dice were controlling me and leading me through the game.

Every time the dice rolled, I landed on different spaces that entitled me to buy property or houses, and go to jail. Every space that I moved to seemed to have a correlation to my different life experiences. When I landed on the Boardwalk, I was given the chance to buy a property on that space, which symbolized the opportunities I have had by joining college access programs like College Bound and the College Crusade of Rhode Island. Just like buying properties helped me win the game, these programs have helped me succeed in high school.

I am proud to be the valedictorian of my senior class and leader in my community. Additionally, sometimes landing on "Chance" meant I had to "Go to Jail." To me, "Going to Jail" signified the obstacles or struggles I have encountered in my life, which I consider to be fate or chance because I was not able to have control over them, like struggling to become valedictorian or trying to be a successful individual coming from an underprivileged city. These among other things, including the death of my grandfather, were all the challenges I had to face during my high school career. On the one hand, the accomplishments I obtained, I consider them personal choice and will because they have allowed me to excel in life.

As I proceeded through the spaces on the game board, I was amazed to see such a strong connection between my life and a common childhood board game. Suddenly, I heard a trembling noise coming from under the game, everything began to shake and the board split into two as if there were some sort of earthquake. I fell through the crevice, and my surroundings disappeared. I heard the familiar voice of my mother calling down to me; I opened my eyes and noticed that I was no longer on the board but back in the basement with the dice at hand and the broken board on the floor. At that that time, it became evident that the dream was no longer surreal; it was reality.

APPENDIX 4

ADDITIONAL PHOTOS

Bryant in front of Brown's Van Wickle Gate on graduation day

Guillermo receiving his diploma from Providence College

Bryant, Theresa, the author, and George

Theresa on the steps of Central Falls High School

Theresa and her friend and pageant mentor, Danielle

George, Theresa, and Bryant on the steps of Central Falls High School

Central Falls High School

Guillermo teaching science to kids at his church's summer school

Acknowledgements

I would first like to thank my editor Kathy Pesta and her husband Michael for their invaluable assistance throughout the writing of *Hope Realized*. Without their expertise in editing and technology, the book would not have reached the level of quality that it has. Kathy is a published author in her own right and spent hours reorganizing and improving my narrative at a time when her own writing agenda was full. I also am most appreciative to Michael who bailed me out of many technological glitches along the way.

Special kudos also go to Judy Robinson for her superb proofreading of my manuscript and to Bill Saslow for his creativeness in designing and producing my book.

Of course, many thanks must go to Bryant, Theresa, Guillermo, and George for their wonderful written contributions to *Hope Realized*. Their personal reflections are insightful and inspiring and comprise the heart of the book. Written in their own words, their stories serve as examples of the fact that it is possible to graduate from a low performing urban high school and not only go to college, but to do well academically.

My deep appreciation also extends to Central Falls principal Josh LaPlante and present and past Central Falls teachers, especially Deloris Grant, Doris White, and Ron Thompson for sharing their love for teaching Central Falls students.

The feedback provided through interviews with college faculty and family members was also invaluable and added much to the book. My sincere thanks go to those people who took time from their busy schedules to provide me with their perceptions of the four students as they observed and interacted with them during their college years.

The information I collected from the *Central Falls High School Third Year Transformation Report* done by the Education Alliance and Annenberg Institute for School Reform at Brown University was particularly helpful in providing me with the current status of reform at the high school and identifying problems still needing to be addressed.

Education writer Linda Borg's articles in the *Providence Journal* on Central Falls and information gathered from *Quality Counts* and *Kids Count* were very useful in my formulation of certain assumptions about the problems and issues that interfere with raising student achievement in inner city schools.

Hope Realized is a very different book from my previous Central Falls book, *A School in Trouble*. My intent was to write a human interest story rather than a traditional education book filled with references, research findings, and quotations. As a result, I depend heavily on my own career experience and feelings and those of parents and college faculty and, of course, the real stars of the book, the four students and the teachers of Central Falls High School.

ABOUT THE AUTHOR

Photo taken by Madison Holland

William R. Holland is a professor emeritus at Rhode Island College and former Rhode Island Commissioner of Higher Education. After beginning his career as a secondary school teacher and administrator, he spent twenty years as a school superintendent in four school districts in Massachusetts and Rhode Island, one of those districts being Central Falls where he was interim superintendent in 2006-2007.

He is the author of four books and numerous journal articles on educational leadership. He and his wife live in Wakefield, Rhode Island. He stays busy doing educational consulting and keeping up with his three children and eight grandchildren.